erasing ED

treatment manual

Tools and Foundations for Eating Disorder Recovery

**By Nicole Laby, MFT, and
Sheira Kahn, MFT**

**With a chapter by
Avril Swan, M.D.**

The companion to
Erasing ED, a documentary
film about recovery from
eating disorders

We dedicate this book to our clients: past, present and future.

CONTENTS

ACKNOWLEDGMENTS

We are grateful to the many people who helped us complete this book. We appreciate Avril Swan, M.D. for contributing her wisdom and knowledge. Many thanks to Christine U'Ren for her copy editing and graphic design talents, and for being such a team player. We are indebted to Ohlhoff Recovery Programs and its staff for providing a training ground where we could meet, learn our craft, and build the foundation for this project. We thank Ed Abramson, Helen Alderson, Pamela Carlton, Marsea Marcus, Anisha Patel-Dunn and Victor Yalom for their professional encouragement and support. We appreciate Phillip Laby for his assistance with the charts and for sharing his business expertise. Thanks also to Diana Zwein for her assistance and dedication.

From Nicole:
First, I am grateful to Sheira Kahn for her invaluable partnership and collaboration in this treatment manual. I extend special thanks to my husband, Phillip Laby, for his support, encouragement, and undying enthusiasm. Thank you Tess and Jackson for your *Wonder-Twin Powers!* I thank my former clients in the documentary *Erasing ED* for providing the inspiration for the film and treatment manual. I am grateful to my current clients for their dedication to recovery. Thanks to Pat Sax and Beth Ohanneson for their warmth and wise words. I have much gratitude for the creation and acceptance of the Expressive Arts in the practice of psychotherapy, and for Sigmund Freud's instrumental work on ego-state development. I am grateful to my family and friends for their continued support of my academic and creative endeavors. And finally, a special thank you to the eating-disorder spe-

cialists at the inpatient unit of Northridge Hospital, where I learned how to recover from my own eating disorder 25 years ago.

From Sheira

Thanks to Nicole Laby for her dedication to the field of eating disorders, her faith in the power of recovery, and her fortitude and grace as a partner. I am grateful to the teachers of the Ridhwan School of Spiritual Development, who both taught and embodied the principles of Superego Disengagement, and who brought me to freedom from my own eating disorder. I thank the staff and clients at La Ventana Eating Disorder Treatment Program, whose enthusiasm and receptivity to the inner-critic work inspired me to bring it to the larger public. I gratefully honor Sigmund Freud for the articulation of his discoveries about the psyche, and the pioneers and proponents of Expressive Arts Therapy as a valid medium of human development. I am indebted to those who encouraged me as a writer, especially Sarah Rose, Philip Jonckheer and Stephanie Moore (of blessed memory). I appreciate my clients, whose devotion to healing never fails to inspire and educate me. I am also grateful to my family and friends for their sustaining love and support.

NOTES

A Note on Language and Gender
Eating disorders affect women and men. Whenever possible, the authors choose gender-neutral language. When gender-specific language is necessary, the authors use "she" and "he" as reflected in the occurrence of eating disorders in the U.S. population, where 90% of the EDs reported are in females, and 10% in males. (Source: www.ANAD.org. Accessed on 12/13/10.)

A Note on the Use of Acronyms
In the eating-disorder field, the acronym "ED" is often used to refer to an eating disorder. Accordingly, the authors refer to eating disorders as "ED" throughout this manual.

Disclaimer
This manual is intended for educational purposes only. It should not take the place of treatment with a licensed professional.

INTRODUCTION

In my extensive research on documentaries related to eating disorders, I discovered there isn't a single film in the United States that is focused *primarily* on treatment techniques and recovery. While some films have elements of recovery in them, most retell the horror stories, leaving the audience with the notion that it is rarely possible to overcome an eating disorder. I am a psychotherapist and consultant in private practice with a specialization in eating disorders, and I directed and produced the documentary *Erasing ED* to promote **recovery**. In my practice, clients followed over a five-year period sustained an 85% recovery rate.[1] The *Erasing ED* documentary and treatment manual is intended as a hands-on, user-friendly training instrument that documents the methods I use.

I collaborated with Sheira Kahn, MFT, and Avril Swan, M.D., so that our combined perspectives would offer the most comprehensive picture of the recovery process. The *Erasing ED Treatment Manual* is a companion to the film, and provides a digest of information on the assessment, diagnosis, medical aspects, etiology, and treatment of eating disorders. Like the film, it is designed to assist mental and physical healthcare providers and trainees in their treatment of eating-disordered clients and patients, but parents, teachers, friends, and those who struggle themselves will also find tools and answers to the mysterious puzzle that is this cluster of illnesses. This manuscript is unique in that it provides (1) a description of concrete interventions

---

1 January 1, 2011 concludes my five-year assessment on current and former clients in recovery from eating disorders. Although I have been treating eating disorders for 17 years, I only began the recovery tracking process five years ago. My next step is to conduct longer follow-up assessments where I can then ascertain recovery status over continuous durations.

along with a comprehensive assessment form that practitioners can use with clients/patients; (2) an understanding of how and why eating disorders form in the psyche based on the principles of ego development; (3) a mock case study and transcribed client session that illustrates how we use the techniques and theory discussed in this manual; and (4) insight into the medical aspects of eating disorders and effective doctor-patient relations.

In her private practice and clinical work, Sheira Kahn, MFT, specializes in helping people take charge of the inner critic — that tyrannical voice that drives ED behaviors. She focuses treatment on the repair of attachment wounds, which she sees as a primary cause of the low self-esteem associated with eating disorders. In addition, Sheira develops continuing education classes based on movies for CEUcinema. com and teaches in the Eating Disorders Certificate Program at UC Berkeley Extension.[2]

Avril Swan, M.D., is a board-certified Family Physician practicing medicine since 2000. She maintains a private practice in San Francisco, where she is also a volunteer Assistant Clinical Professor with the University of California, San Francisco. She devotes a substantial portion of her practice to the diagnosis and treatment of people with eating disorders. She also gives talks to other physicians, medical students and public school children about eating disorders.

Recovery does not have to be a mystery. We have found instead that, through the use of these techniques, it becomes a concrete process involving the application of ego-state intervention and reconstitution. Thank you for your interest and participation in erasing eating disorders.

Nicole Laby, MFT

---

2 Continuing Education units are available for watching *Erasing ED* and reading this manual at www.ceucinema.com. For more information on *Erasing ED*, go to www.ErasingED.com.

CO-AUTHOR'S NOTE

For decades, the best practice in eating-disorder research and writing was to say that the causes are unknown. This is changing. We live in an exciting time when the revelations of the early pioneers of psychotherapy and the recent research on attachment have dovetailed, finally giving us much-needed answers to the mystery of eating disorders and their treatment.

Nicole Laby and I benefitted as those revelations were developed into the concrete interventions we used to recover from our own eating disorders. We have updated them, adding our personal understanding as practitioners, for inclusion in this manual.

Sheira Kahn, MFT

Part One

Plate 1: *Smothering*

I am lost.
You promise life so I
construct a thousand rings.
I cast them into the deep and hang on, barely.
I manufacture one thousand more.
Still you drown me.

CHAPTER 1

Comprehensive Guide to Diagnosis and Assessment

This chapter will focus on the *DSM-IV* (*Diagnostic and Statistical Manual – Fourth Edition*) criteria for eating disorders and the comprehensive assessment required to collect vital client history and determine a diagnosis.

Diagnosis: *DSM-IV* Criteria

Three eating-disorder diagnoses are featured in the *DSM-IV*: (1) Anorexia Nervosa, (2) Bulimia Nervosa, and (3) Eating Disorder Not Otherwise Specified (EDNOS). Definitions, diagnostic criteria and codes are detailed below.

Anorexia Nervosa: 307.1

This disorder is marked by the refusal to sustain an appropriate and normal body weight. The diagnosis is given when one's weight falls below 85% of what is considered normal for one's age and height, according to established growth charts. The *DSM-IV* stipulates that anorexics "…refuse to maintain a minimally normal body weight, are intensely afraid of gaining weight, and exhibit a significant disturbance in the perception of shape or size of his/her body." In post-menarcheal females, amenorrhea may occur (i.e., at least three consecutive menstrual cycles are nonexistent).

Subtypes of Anorexia:
- Restricting Type: The individual demonstrates weight loss through diets, fasts, and compulsive exercise. The individual does not consistently engage in binge eating or purging behaviors (see list of purging behaviors below).
- Binge-Eating/Purging Type: In addition to food restriction, dieting, and fasting, the individual consistently engages in binge-eating or purging behaviors, including compulsive exercise, self-induced vomiting, laxative abuse, diuretic abuse, or enema abuse.

Bulimia Nervosa: 307.51
This disorder is characterized by binge eating[3] followed by purging behaviors. The *DSM-IV* suggests that the purging behaviors or "inappropriate compensatory methods" are constructed by the individual in order to avoid weight gain. Additionally, the body size and shape is of critical importance to the individual and she becomes obsessed about it, weighing herself and body-checking multiple times a day. For bulimia to be diagnosed, these behaviors must occur at least twice a week for a minimum of three months. Other diagnostic features include an absence of control associated with eating-disordered behaviors, and an inability to stop and/or monitor food intake.

Subtypes of Bulimia:
- Purging Type: Individuals consistently engage in the following types of compensatory behaviors: self-induced vomiting, laxative abuse, diuretic abuse, or enema abuse.

---

3 Binge eating is defined as excessive caloric intake that occurs in two hours or less; food intake is grossly larger than the average portion consumed by someone who does not have an eating disorder.

- Non-Purging Type: Individuals utilize fasting, dieting, and/or compulsive exercise to compensate for binge eating; they do not frequently engage in self-induced vomiting, laxative abuse, diuretic abuse, or enema abuse.

Eating Disorder Not Otherwise Specified 307.50

This diagnosis is for eating disorders that do not satisfy the criteria for either Anorexia Nervosa or Bulimia Nervosa. Individuals with EDNOS can present with features from different eating disorders. At the time of this writing, there is no specific diagnosis for compulsive or binge eating without compensatory behaviors in the *DSM-IV*. (See below.)

Diagnostic Criteria:
- The individual engages in binge eating, but does not engage in any inappropriate compensatory behaviors.[4]
- Females exhibit all behaviors and criteria under Anorexia Nervosa, but regular menses continue to exist.
- The individual maintains a normal body weight even though all criteria are met for Anorexia Nervosa.
- The individual meets all criteria for Bulimia Nervosa, but the frequency and duration of behaviors is less than twice a week and/or less than a three-month period.
- Inappropriate compensatory behaviors occur after the individual consumes small amounts of food.
- The individual chews and spits repeatedly, without ingesting any of the food.

Assessment

The **Comprehensive Eating-Disorder Assessment** has fifteen parts and can be found in Appendix A. The following identifies and illustrates each part.

---

4 Although it does not appear in the *DSM-IV* alongside anorexia and bulimia, "Binge eating is on track to become a formal psychiatric diagnosis," (John Gaver, Senior Editor, *MedPage Today*; http://www.health.am/psy/more/obesity-rejected-as-psychiatric-diagnosis-in-dsm-5/) and is currently listed as an appendix in the *DSM-IV*.

1. Client Demographics

A detailed list of demographics provides a picture of the client's overall psycho-social life and health. It is also helpful to have this information on hand for reference during treatment. This section includes the following:

- Name
- Date of assessment
- Age
- Date of birth
- Gender
- Ethnicity
- Sexual orientation
- Employment and/or school
- Primary source of income
- Insurance information (if applicable)
- Relationship status
- Referral source
- Client contact and emergency contact information
- Multi-axial diagnosis

2. Treatment History

The treatment history directly impacts how you will work with the individual and how you will arrive at a diagnosis. This section should contain a detailed record of past and current treatment, as well as the duration of each treatment episode. Note that an inquiry about the Twelve Steps is included, as some individuals use various Twelve-Step programs for support in ED and other kinds of recovery. Include the following:

- Psychiatrists
- Psychologists
- Psychotherapists
- Social workers
- Dieticians
- Intensive outpatient programs (IOP)
- Partial hospitalization programs (PHP)

- Residential programs and hospitalizations
- Twelve-Step experience

Later you will obtain the client's permission to exchange information with practitioners whose work pertains to current treatment.

3. *Medical History*

Eating-disordered individuals are frequently burdened by their shame and may neglect to disclose their ED to their doctors or visit a doctor for fear of judgment. By obtaining the following information you will better understand the individual's health history and status:

- Name of medical doctor
- List of medication(s) and doses
- Significant medical history
- Date of last menses
- Date of last doctor's appointment and reason for the appointment
- Does the previous doctor know about the individual's eating issues/behaviors?
- Date of last dental appointment
- Does the dentist know about the client's eating issues/behaviors?

4. *Self-harm and Violence History*

In this section, the focus is on behaviors and cognitions. Self-harm can manifest as cutting, burning, hitting, pulling out hair, biting, and the like. Although eating-disorder behaviors are also self-harming, the interest here is in behaviors that aren't ED-related. Include dates of occurrence as you record the following:

- Self-harming behaviors
- Suicidal ideation
- Suicide attempts
- Homicidal ideation
- Violence toward others

5. *Abuse History*

Bedside manner is vital when collecting information of this nature. Individuals with a history of abuse may often feel terrified to discuss or disclose for fear of judgment and/or recapitulating the painful events. You might be the first person in whom the individual confides regarding his/her abuse history. We strongly advise that the healthcare provider facilitate questions and reactions to answers with compassion, appropriate boundaries, and acceptance. Include dates of occurrence as you record the following:

- Emotional or verbal abuse
- Physical abuse
- Sexual abuse: rape and/or date rape
- Domestic violence

> Look for instances of abandonment or emotional neglect. A parent who is physically present can nonetheless leave a child with "relationship PTSD" if that parent is narcissistic and/or emotionally unavailable.[5]

6. *Specific Eating Disorder Information and Behaviors*

This section will provide the specific criteria for diagnosis. Obtain the following information:

- Present weight and height:
    —Highest weight and age
    —Lowest weight and age (lowest adult weight if treating an adult)
    —Individual's report of "ideal" weight (this helps to discern body-image distortion)
    —Frequency of weighing self

---

5 For further information, see note on "Narcissism: The Other Killer" in Chapter 3.

When inquiring about highest and lowest weight, also ask what was happening in the person's life during that time. This will help you identify how the eating disorder is impacted by circumstances and your client's reaction to them.

- Eating-disorder-related complications that impact physical health (e.g., acid reflux, blood in vomit or stool, etc.)
- Description of binges: food content, where and when binges occur (alone or in public)
- List of "safe" foods (i.e., foods that won't trigger binges/purges; foods that are tolerable for those who restrict and struggle with eating)
- Current and past behaviors (inquire as to the individual's engagement in the following):
    —Binge eating
    —Compulsive overeating[6]
    —Restricting[7]
    —Fasting (such as a "juice only" fast)
    —Dieting
    —Diet pills
    —Vomiting
    —Laxative use
    —Diuretics
    —Supplements
    —Enemas
    —Ipecac use (to induce vomiting)
    —Compulsive exercise (frequency, intensity, and duration; and is it compensatory?)
    —Chewing and spitting

---

6 Compulsive overeating does not constitute a binge. The quantity of caloric consumption is less. Both clients who binge and those who eat compulsively without bingeing report feeling "out-of-control."

7 Restricting involves eating small amounts of food over the course of a day.

—Eating late at night/in the middle of the night
—Hoarding or hiding food
—Counting calories/making caloric lists
—Cutting food into small pieces
—Creating rules and/or rituals when to eat
—Frequently weighing oneself
—Preoccupation with body weight and size
—Eating an ultra-pure diet (e.g., restricting fats, proteins, and carbohydrates and only eating vegetables, fruits, etc.)

Sometimes a compulsive exerciser will withdraw entirely from this behavior. Similarly, a client may suddenly stop restricting and give himself permission to eat taboo foods. This is the id's effort to rebel against the superego and is a sign that the client is surrendering to recovery.

After obtaining the list of current and past behaviors above, simplify this into a list of behaviors and frequency of behaviors that occurred in the **past six months**, and then those that occurred in the **past month**. This information will assist you in arriving at a diagnosis.

7. Family History

Eating disorders typically develop out of the dynamics within a family system, so information on family relationships is essential. Additionally, a family history of eating disorders is important, as EDs can occur transgenerationally. Records of chemical dependency and mental illness are also relevant, as these conditions affect psychological development and can impact eating disorders. Obtain a list of other illnesses, including the following, and the family members who have or had them:

- Eating disorders
- Chemical dependency and/or abuse
- Mental health issues or illness
- Physical illness

- Genogram[8] (If time is limited, do a brief genogram of immediate family only.)

8. Onset and Duration of Eating Disorder

This is a detailed description of the individual's report of when and why the eating disorder began. Sometimes people will have periods of remission from the eating disorder and/or periods of extreme frequency of symptoms. To get a complete picture of the eating disorder, remark on the full spectrum of behaviors, including any shifts or changes in the eating disorder that occurred over time.

9. List of Food Consumed on a Typical Day

This question is placed later in the assessment, as most people with EDs report enormous shame when detailing their food consumption. Therefore, it is best to ask this information once a rapport is established. Obtain the following information: date, time, food content, and quantity (of food consumed for each meal/snack/episode). This information can illuminate restricting and/or bingeing behaviors and patterns. Additionally, it can help to identify physical versus emotional hunger.[9]

10. Chemical Dependency (CD) History

The individual can suffer a comorbid condition involving both chemical dependency and eating disorders. Additionally, drugs and alcohol can trigger eating-disorder behaviors. When a comor-

---

8 A genogram is a diagram of the client's family tree, including names/ages/occupations/school status of family members; interpersonal connections between family members; mental illnesses, eating disorders and/or other addictions, etc. If you need help constructing a genogram, go to http://www.genopro.com/genogram/rules/

9 Physical hunger is true hunger the body feels and is not influenced by one's emotional state. Emotional hunger is often disguised as physical hunger. Emotional hunger is merely the psyche's attempt to express difficult emotions. The ED attempts to satisfy emotional hunger through binges or compulsive eating. Adding a further twist to the original experience, some people attempt to satisfy emotional hunger (or deprivation) through restricting.

bid (or dual) diagnosis[10] exists and the chemical dependency is chronic, CD treatment will take priority. Obtain a list of the following substance use:

- Name of substance(s) including all alcohol and drugs
- Duration of use, including frequency and greatest amounts consumed
- Last use date and amount

11. *History of Other Compulsive Behaviors*

This section includes sex and love addiction, gambling addiction, excessive spending, debting, underspending, self-deprivation, and any behavior that exhibits the lack of impulse control. Include the duration and frequency of each behavior. Some clients engage in these types of behaviors when the ED is less symptomatic. It is important to be aware of all compulsive behaviors in order to best serve the client.

12. *Support System*

Individuals with eating disorders are often initially secretive about the disorder and lack emotional support. The fear of judgment frequently overrides their ability to reach out to loved ones; some family and friends might not understand eating disorders. Others may not be qualified as supporters due to family dysfunction. Obtain a list of family and/or friends with whom the individual feels safe and supported, along with a list of anyone who knows about his/her eating disorder (and substance abuse, if applicable).

13. *Client's Expectations of Treatment*

Discuss and record the individual's expectation of treatment, including what he wants to change as a result of treatment and what he hopes to accomplish.

---

10 In some treatment centers, "dual diagnosis" refers to eating disorders and chemical dependency. In other treatment centers, "dual diagnosis" refers to chemical dependency and mental illness.

14. Result of Interview/Clinician's Recommendations

In this section, report your findings, including diagnosis, clinical suggestions, and concerns.

15. Release of Confidentiality

Obtain permission from the client to share information with other members of the treatment team. Working within a group is not only best for the client, it also distributes the responsibility of providing care among parents, partners, loved ones and clinicians, so no single person becomes overwhelmed.

Teens with eating disorders are often hesitant to share their recovery with a parent or caregiver, so be sure to review your policy on confidentiality and stick to it when working with a minor. In enmeshed family systems, it is often in the teen's best interest to secure and uphold boundaries related to confidentiality, so that parents are less inclined to undermine the client-therapist relationship. This can be difficult for the parent, but the treatment team will assist in quelling this anxiety.

See Appendix A for a usable copy of this assessment form.

CHAPTER 2

Medical Aspects of Eating Disorders

The primary care provider, whether physician, nurse practitioner, or physician's assistant, is often in the position of coordinating care and directing the patient to appropriate treatment resources in the community. It is important to feel comfortable knowing when to refer the person with an eating disorder from outpatient services to a higher level of care based on her psychiatric and medical status. The following article was designed to give you information on providing medical attention and management, determining the patient's overall medical needs, and making psychiatric and other referrals.

How Common Are Eating Disorders?

The reported lifetime incidence of Anorexia Nervosa is .3–3.7% of females and .2–.3% of males. These numbers almost surely underreport the true incidence, as many patients never come to medical attention. Bulimia is more common, with a lifetime incidence of 1–4.2%. Eating Disorder Not Otherwise Specified is thought to be the most common eating disorder of all, comprising between 50–75% of eating-disorder treatment populations. (Williams, Goodie, & Motsinger, 2008)

Therapeutic Alliance

Clinicians treating eating disorders cannot help patients medically unless they develop a therapeutic alliance. Reassuring the patients that you are there to support them, not judge them, is essential to gaining trust. Be sure, as you are forming an alliance, that you:

- Never assume a patient does or does not have an eating disorder based on appearance.
- Refrain from commenting on appearance and weight.
- Examine your own beliefs about eating disorders and put your judgment aside. Remember that eating disorders are not the fault of the patient. Treat ED patients as you would treat any other patient: with care, compassion and kindness.
- Ask patients how *they* feel about their body, their nutrition, and their weight.
- Make screening for eating disorders part of your regular review of systems. (See the comprehensive ED Assessment described in Chapter 1.)

Why Do People Get Eating Disorders?

Current research supports a combination of genetic and biological reasons, together with personal attributes and environmental contributions. (Birmingham & Treasure, 2010)

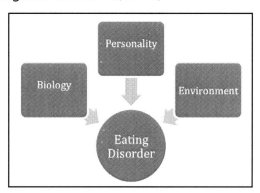

For a more detailed explanation of causes, please see Chapter 3.

Medical Complications

Eating disorders are multisystemic illnesses. While a patient may appear stable at one sitting, it only takes a short time for serious consequences to develop. It is important that the clinician be on the lookout for changes in mental status, including suicidal behaviors and thoughts, as well as changes in physical status. A physical exam must be done each time you see the patient. Similarly, vital signs, including weight, orthostatic blood pressure, and heart rate, must be monitored at every visit.

Medical complications may include the following (American Academy of Pediatrics, 2003)(APA, 2006):

- **General**: dehydration, malnutrition, electrolyte imbalances, hypercarotenemia, re-feeding syndrome
- **Cardiac**: arrhythmias, EKG abnormalities, sudden death, mitral valve prolapse
- **Skin problems**: rashes, dry skin, worsening eczema, easy bruising and bleeding, hair loss
- **Endocrine**: amenorrhea, high cholesterol, high cortisol, low blood sugar, infertility, diabetes insipidus, osteoporosis, euthyroid sick syndrome
- **Gastrointestinal (GI)**: esophageal rupture, gastritis, esophagitis, Mallory Weiss tears, parotid disease, pancreatitis, constipation, abnormal liver function
- **Hematologic**: anemia, neutropenia, thrombocytopenia
- **Neurologic**: memory and cognition problems, seizures, neuropathies
- **Pulmonary**: rib fractures, worse outcome with bacterial pneumonia, aspiration syndrome
- **Renal**: kidney stones
- **Dental**: tooth decay and erosion

Taking the History

The history of present illness as it relates to eating disorders should include the following (American Academy of Pediatrics, 2003) (Birmingham & Treasure, 2010):

- Greatest and least weight (and height if the patient is an adolescent)
- Patient's desired weight
- Exercise: how much, how often, and level of intensity
- Is exercise compensatory in nature? (e.g., after a binge)

Current Dietary Practices

- 24-hour recall of amounts and types of food and fluids — does this reflect a typical 24 hours?
- Food restrictions or taboo foods

Current and Past History of Eating Disorder

- Current and past food restricting
- Current and past history of binge eating and purging: frequency, amount, and triggers
- Use of diuretics, laxatives, diet pills, ipecac

Current and Past Medical/Psychiatric History

(Birmingham & Treasure, 2010)

- Current treatment by psychiatrist and/or therapist?
- Has the patient had any previous therapy for eating disorders? What kind and how long?
- Any hospitalizations or ER visits?
- Any history of other psychiatric illnesses?
- Any birth trauma or serious childhood illnesses?
- Any suicidal ideation or intent?

Family History

Ask the patient if parents or other family members have experienced any of the following:

- Obesity
- Eating disorders

- Depression
- Other mental illness
- Substance abuse

Social History
Inquire and document:
- Use of cigarettes, drugs, and alcohol
- Sexual history
- History of physical or sexual abuse

Review of Systems
- **General**: thinking difficulties, poor memory, fatigue, frequent illness, weight loss or gain, night sweats
- **Endocrine:** cold intolerance, frequent thirst
- **Hematologic:** pallor, bruising, bleeding
- **Neurologic:** dizziness, syncope or pre-syncope, headaches, double vision
- **Skin/hair**: hair loss, lanugo, dry skin, poor healing
- **GI**: vomiting, diarrhea, constipation, fullness, bloating, abdominal pain, epigastric burning
- **Musculoskeletal**: muscle cramps, joint pain, fractures
- **Reproductive**: menstrual history, including age of menarche, cycle regularity, and last menstrual period.

Physical Exam
A physical exam should be performed after a review of systems at every visit. The physical exam should occur in a dressing gown and should always include weight after the patient provides a urine specimen. The urine specimen can be used, if needed, to check specific gravity to preclude water-loading, and ensures that the patient is providing a dry weight. Usually the patient should not be permitted to know the weight until her recovery is solid and she doesn't get preoccupied or "triggered" by the number on the scale. This is called a "blind weigh-in." (Society for Adolescent Medicine, 2003) (APA, 2006) (5) (American Academy of Pediatrics, 2003)

Vital Signs

Though there can be great variation depending on the age and physical condition of the patient, the following list provides general guidelines of abnormal vital signs that may require acute hospitalization (Society for Adolescent Medicine, 2003):

- **Heart rate**: < 50 BPM (Beats Per Minute) in adolescents and < 40 in adults
- **Blood pressure**: < 80/50
- **Orthostatic changes**: greater than 20 BPM pulse or greater than 20 mm hg
- **Temperature**: < 96°F
- **Weight**: Body Mass Index (BMI) < 85% of ideal body weight or < 75% of average body weight for age, sex, height

> **Adult BMI calculator**: http://www.cdc.gov/healthy-weight/assessing/bmi/adult_bmi/english_bmi_calculator/bmi_calculator.html

> **Child and adolescent BMI calculator**: http://apps.nccd.cdc.gov/dnpabmi/

Common Physical Findings

- **General**: under or overweight
- **Head and neck**: swollen and/or tender parotid glands, poor dentition, palatal petechiae, dehydrated mucous membranes and dry lips, circles under the eyes
- **Cardiac**: bradycardia, hypotension, tachycardia
- **Skin**: dry skin, Russell's sign (calluses on dorsum of the hand), slow-healing wounds, evidence of cutting on arms and legs, ecchymoses
- **Extremities**: cool extremities, acrocyanosis, mild edema, painful and/or swollen foot (stress fracture)

Less Common Findings

- **Cardiac**: heart murmur or midsystolic click (mitral valve prolapse), evidence of heart failure (jugular venous distension, S3, severe edema, pulmonary edema, palpable liver or ascites)
- **Skin**: lanugo, pressure sores, hair loss

Laboratory Testing

Patients who are actively engaging in eating-disorder behaviors risk electrolyte imbalance, cardiac damage, seizures, and endocrine and hematologic abnormalities. Though most laboratory assessments are normal, normal lab results do not preclude serious illness or medical instability (American Academy of Pediatrics, 2003).

Initial laboratory work should include the following: complete blood count, electrolyte measurement, liver function tests, serum phosphorous, serum or red blood cell magnesium, vitamin B_{12}, vitamin D, thyroid function tests, sedimentation rate, urinalysis, and in women or adolescent females, a pregnancy test. If there is any arrhythmia, including bradycardia or tachycardia, or any cardiac symptoms, an EKG should be performed. If a post-menarcheal female hasn't had a menstrual period for six or more months, a bone densitometry should be performed (American Academy of Pediatrics, 2003).

Referring to Higher Level of Care

If, in your outpatient practice, a patient is medically unstable — meaning vital signs are in a dangerous range or electrolytes need rapid correcting, suicidality is present, or there is a medical condition that needs monitoring such as a cardiac arrhythmia, GI bleed, or severe malnutrition — inpatient hospitalization is necessary. If the medical condition isn't that serious, but the patient isn't making progress with the outpatient team or seems to be taking a turn for the worse, then a higher level of care is needed. This may mean intensive outpatient care, partial hospitalization, or residential care. The decision as to the level of care frequently depends on what is available, affordable, and accessible. Residential treatment is generally reserved for medically stable individuals who are nevertheless compromised psychiatrically and have poor-to-fair motivation and a need for highly structured supervision of all meals and activities. Because of your role as a co-ordinator of the overall care for a patient with an eating disorder, it is important for you to know the names of several psychiatrists, thera-pists, and registered dieticians whom you trust (Williams, Goodie, & Motsinger, 2008).

Conclusion
Eating disorders are real medical illnesses with high morbidity and mortality. A therapeutic alliance, together with careful consideration of the physical and emotional state of your patient, will contribute a tremendous amount to her safety, well-being, and recovery.

References

American Academy of Pediatrics. Identifying and Treating Eating Dis-orders: Policy Statement from the Committee on Adolescence. *Pedi-atrics.* 2003;111:204-211.

American Psychiatric Association website. *APA Practice Guidelines 2006: Treatment of Patients with Eating Disorders.* Available at http://www.psychiatryonline.com/content.aspx?aID=139788. Accessed: November 9, 2010.

Birmingham CL, Treasure J. *Medical Management of Eating Disorders.* Cambridge, UK; Cambridge University Press, 2010.

Button EJ, Bhanu C, Palmer RL. Mortality and Predictors of Death in a Cohort of Patients Presenting to an Eating Disorder Service. *Interna-tional Journal of Eating Disorders.* 2010; 43: 387-392

Mehler PS, Birmingham CL, Crow SJ, et al. Medical Complications of Eating Disorders. In: Grilo CM, Mitchell JE, eds. *The Treatment of Eat-ing Disorders: A Clinical Handbook:* New York, New York: Guilford Press; 2010:66-80

Mitchell JE, Crow S, Medical Complications of Anorexia Nervosa and Bulimia Nervosa. *Current Opinion in Psychiatry.* 2006;19:438-443.

National Alliance of Mental Illness website. *Eating Disorder Not Otherwise Specified.* Available at http://www.nami.org/Template. cfm?Section=By_Illness&template=/ContentManagement/Content-Display.cfm&ContentID=65849 Accessed November 11, 2010.

Society for Adolescent Medicine. Eating Disorders in Adolescents: Position Paper of the Society for Adolescent Medicine. *Journal of Adolescent Health.* 2003;33:496-503.

Williams PM, Goodie J, Motsinger CD. Treating Eating Disorders in Primary Care. *American Family Physician.* 2008;77:187-195

Part Two

Plate 2: *Ontogeny*

Are you part of my herd?
You sear.
You brand, prod, and scatter,
But you don't own.
I recognize you, but can't place your face.
Order or chaos?
And which one am I?

CHAPTER 3

Hijacked by Shame: The Etiology of Eating Disorders

Hijacked by Shame: The World Inside

Family, friends, professionals, even eating-disorder sufferers themselves find eating disorders perplexing. Why would an otherwise intelligent and competent woman refuse to do the most basic thing
to keep herself alive — to eat, or refrain from overeating if that were
threatening her health? While the behaviors do not seem logical, they
do make sense in the context of the eating-disorder sufferer's inner
world.[11]

The inner world of someone with an eating disorder is constantly
being hijacked by self-hatred and shame. Although we've all experienced shame, few people who have not had an eating disorder can
imagine the intensity of the shame for someone who has. Recall your
most excruciating, humiliating memory. Were you panicked? Did
you want to escape? Were you so desperate in that moment that dy-

---

11   A note on gender: Eating disorders affect women and men. Whenever possible,
the authors choose gender-neutral language. When gender-specific language is
necessary, the authors use "she" and "he" as reflected in the occurrence of eating
disorders in the U.S. population, where 90% of the EDs reported are found in
females, and 10% in males. (Source: www.ANAD.org. Accessed December 14, 2010.)

ing seemed preferable? You have barely begun to experience what someone in the throes of an eating disorder deals with continuously. Triggers are everywhere, from the number on the scale, to a brief glance in the mirror, to the perception that she said the wrong thing to someone.

People with eating disorders are often intelligent and passionate. The part of the psyche that creates the shame fuses this intelligence and passion to create a conviction of failure so strong that the ED sufferer experiences it at a cellular level. Because it feels authentic, questioning the conviction would be inaccurate, disobedient — even blasphemous. In this way, the shame hijacks her body, her mind and her emotions.

For example, take the assertion, "You're fat." Imagine that a well-nourished, but not overweight person is continually hearing that statement echo in her mind. She compares herself to models such as Gisele Bündchen, Kate Moss, and Niki Taylor — all of whom met the physical criteria for anorexia at the time of this writing.[12] Strictly speaking, if that is the standard to which she is comparing herself, indeed she is "fat." Her intelligence then tells her that the assertion "You're fat" is accurate. This leads to despair, which she experiences as real because her passionate nature allows her to feel things deeply and directly.

The shame leads to a further conclusion: "Because you are fat, you are unlovable." This produces such a desperate feeling of isolation and failure that the person would do anything — ANYTHING — to improve the situation. The easiest thing to control is her body, so the dagger of shame turns inward. The depth of the conviction that she is unlovable, corroborated by emotions that feel true at a cellular level, combine to make her want to die rather than eat or gain weight. (Conversely, the person may be dying TO eat as an escape from the desperate feelings inside.) What she is trying to control is not just her body, but also her intolerable sense of isolation and failure. Unfortunately, the eating disorder only magnifies what it seeks to assuage, since it amplifies her sense of weakness and despicability. (For more

---

12   Source: http://www.raderprograms.com/causes-statistics/media-eating-disorders.html. Accessed December 14, 2010.

information on how the eating disorder magnifies the pain, please see "The Eating Disorder Cycle" section in Chapter 5.)

The Hijacker Uncovered

The shame and obsessive ED thoughts are best understood and treated through the lens of Freud's descriptions of the psyche.[13] A battle rages between the part of the person that naturally wants to eat, and the part that wants him not to. The battle is slightly different in each type of eating disorder. The way the battle unfolds determines what kind of eating disorder each person will have. The three main types — anorexia, bulimia, and binge eating — are described below, preceded by a brief review of Freudian psychology to clarify terms.

Freud understood the human psyche to be comprised of three main, interactive elements: the ego, superego, and id. These elements are not permanently fixed. They act as processes and function together harmoniously or not, depending upon the health of the system. Here is a brief description of each:[14]

- **"Ego"** means "I" in Latin, and is the central identity or sense of self. The ego is the seat of consciousness, and includes perceptual, intellectual, and executive functions. It organizes us to learn language, drive a car, and sort out sensory input. The ego's main function is to **oversee, mediate,** and **house** the different elements of the psyche.
- **"Superego"** in Latin means "over-I." The superego's main job is to protect and guide the ego. It does this by providing **information, regulations** and **boundaries**. The superego is conceptualized as a person's conscience. It is the moralizing and critical part of the psyche (hence its interchangeability with the term "inner critic").

---

13 The authors of this manual do not consider themselves "Freudians" per se, but find his model useful for the etiology of eating disorders.

14 For a complete description of these terms, the authors recommend Calvin Hall's *Primer of Freudian Psychology,* cited in the next footnote.

- **"Id"** has been translated from the German word "es" for "it." The id is the seat of the instincts, supplying to the system messages about physical and emotional needs. It is associated with the child part of a human being. The id's main job is to **supply psychic energy** to the rest of the system.

In a healthy person, "…these three systems form a unified and harmonious organization. By working together cooperatively, they enable the individual to carry on efficient and satisfying transactions with his environment."[15] In this scenario, the ego reigns. It has wide and flexible — but reliable — boundaries, allowing a variety of emotions, beliefs, and experiences to be included in the person's central identity. The superego and the id cooperate in service of the ego (see Diagram 1, "The Healthy Psyche"). The superego provides gentle reminders and boundaries that help a person take care of himself and fit in with society, such as "Study hard so you can get into a good school." The id supplies messages about survival such as, "I am hungry. It's time to eat," and "I am lonely." In a healthy person, the urges and needs of the id, both physical and emotional, are welcomed and heeded by the ego. Conflict is minimal.

---

15 Hall, Calvin S., *A Primer of Freudian Psychology* (New York: New American Library, 1954), 22.

Diagram 1
The Healthy Psyche

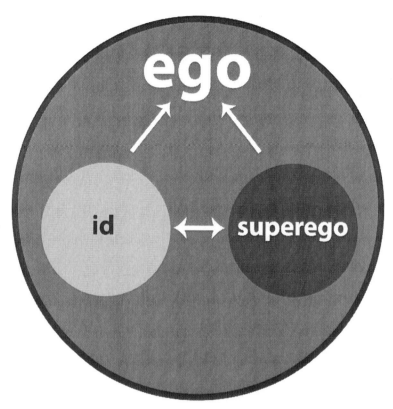

Id and superego work together in support of the ego. There is a clear boundary around the ego, indicating integrity within the system. The id and superego are in balance with each other. The ego holds most of the psychic energy.

When these three systems are not working together, the person "…is dissatisfied with himself and the world, and his efficiency is reduced."[16] Eating disorders are an extreme example of this. While some mentally unhealthy people are dominated by the id, people with eating disorders tend to be dominated by a tyrannical superego that battles the id, leaving the ego narrow and powerless (see Diagram 2, "The Unhealthy Psyche"), destroying the life force of the person it is trying to protect. A large number of feelings and experiences are excluded from the central identity, even common ones such as sadness and vulnerability. Instead of "study hard," the superego in someone with an ED would say "You had better work your butt off to try and muster a decent grade because FAT CHANCE you will even pass this test, let alone get into a good school, MORON!" In this environment, when the id comes forward with its message of "I'm hungry," the superego spews rejection and derision in words or via a silent, toxic energy: "You are disgusting and unlovable! Not another bite until you lose ten pounds, PIG!" The unhealthy superego hijacks all the emotional energy from the id and becomes inflated and blustery, leaving the ego contracted and depleted, with the id fighting just to stay on the radar.

> The id has at times been construed, in earlier psychological literature and in society at large, as a hostile force that must be tamed. Yet the id plays a crucial role in human health as the supplier of psychic energy. No human can survive without it. This is why the perfectionism of eating disorders (perfectionism being an effort to satisfy the superego) becomes lethal. Freud is quoted as saying that suicide was an unhealthy prevalence of the "Over-I" in the system.[17] When the id energy is gone, so is the life force and the will to live. At that point, self-starvation makes sense. Alternatively, the aggressive superego can force the id to get its needs met only through hostile takeovers of the psyche, resulting in bingeing or binge-purge behaviors, which can also be lethal.

---

16 Ibid.
17 Edmundson, Mark, *The Death of Sigmund Freud* (New York: Bloomsbury, 2007), 86.

Another aspect of the unhealthy psyche is that the superego and id can collude and destroy the ego — or seek to destroy another person. In this scenario, the caustic criticisms of the superego join forces with the raw energy of the id to direct hatred toward the identified enemy, whether it is the ED client herself or someone else. Each person's process is different, so it is important to discern how this occurs for each individual. (The id/superego relationship becomes especially important as you create the treatment plan and choose interventions.)

Whether in conflict with each other or in collusion against a perceived enemy, the antagonized superego and id consume most of the person's psychic energy and time, with little left over for the development of a sense of self or ego. The result is that what is acceptable to feel, say, and do, i.e., what is allowed to be part of the conscious self, is severely limited for people with eating disorders. (This is another way of understanding the low self-esteem in people with EDs.) Those limitations force eating-disorder sufferers into psychic territory where typical human feelings are met with the superego's harsh criticism (hence the alternate name for the superego, "inner critic"). At that point, the part that houses the emotions, the id, may wake up and seek relief from the intolerable pain of the superego's abuse. This relief is sought in the form of food, exercise, or restricting. In order for its urges to be heard, the id must be loud and forceful. The id's force only escalates the conflict with the superego, however, and a full-blown battle ensues.

Diagram 2a
The Unhealthy Psyche - I

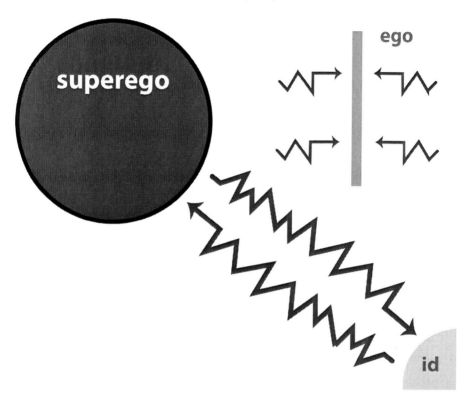

The superego antagonizes the id, attempting to banish it from the system. The ego is narrow and has no energy for standing up to the superego. The superego holds most of the psychic energy.

Diagram 2b
The Unhealthy Psyche - II

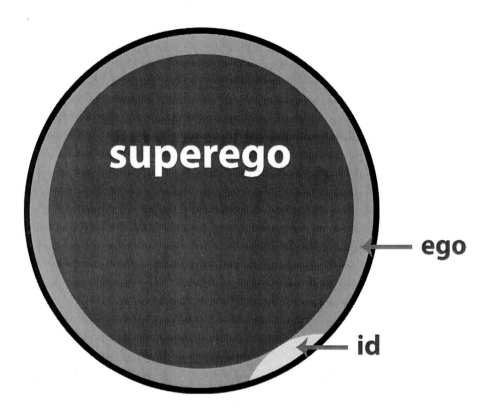

This diagram illustrates a second way to conceptualize the unhealthy psyche. The superego takes up most of the psychic energy, leaving but a narrow band for the ego and an even smaller portion for the id.

Body as Battleground
In all three eating-disorder types, the body is the battleground in the conflict between the id and the superego, and food (restriction or consumption) is the ammunition. Each type of eating disorder is an expression of what is happening in the person's psyche. The eating-disorder behaviors are a manifestation of the superego combating the id; the quest for a thin body is an externalization of the internal sense of a small and narrow ego. This is why it is important to conceptualize and treat eating disorders as mental illnesses with physical consequences, not as physical illnesses with mental consequences.

Anorexia
The superego has won the battle in people with anorexia so that they cannot hear the id's urges and messages to eat. By restricting, they have "succeeded" in the eyes of the superego. All of their emotional energy and life force, when it comes to food, is housed in the superego. If they have an urge to eat, they refrain from food, channeling the energy instead into a "superego-approved" activity such as exercising.

When anorexics have satisfied the superego by restricting or doing something else of its bidding, they report feeling powerful since the superego has mastered its objective: obedience. Now that the ego obeys and the id has been slain, there is nothing on the horizon BUT superego, and the client begins to identify herself as the superego. This leaves the anorexic with a sense of superiority over others because she can do what they cannot: she can rise above her human needs. The identification with the superego serves to illustrate how eating disorders are mental illnesses with physical consequences: when the superego is "successful" at killing off the id, the body begins to die.

Bulimia
For bulimics, the superego reigns supreme, with episodes of the id fighting its way in for a brief takeover before the superego is victorious once more. Many bulimics report a period of being "good" with

food, meaning that they have satisfied the edicts of the superego, quashed the id, and are restricting or compensating for having eaten. In contrast to anorexics, however, bulimics cannot banish the urges of the id completely. "I am hungry. I want pancakes," says the id. The superego replies, "You can't have pancakes. You had bread last night for dinner." "But I'm *hungry*," the id insists, escalating the fight. At some point, the id wins and a binge begins. People report an experience of a runaway train, as they cram everything they can into their mouths while they are still saying "yes" to food.

While people who don't have eating disorders see eating as healthy and necessary, bulimics feel differently (in part because of the out-of-control element associated with eating). Once they are being "good" again, giving in to the id by eating is seen as a complete failure and bulimics hate themselves for bingeing.

Binge-eating disorder
For binge eaters, the id is winning the battle between id and superego when it comes to food. Like people with anorexia and bulimia, many binge eaters start the day by restricting. As they become physically hungry, or begin to crave food simply because they are set up by the injunction that they shouldn't have it, the conflict between id and superego escalates, just as it does for bulimics. "I'm hungry," says the id. "Well no one likes you this way. Don't eat!" replies the superego. "But I'm HUNGRY!" insists the id. As the fight heats up, the id's urges get stronger until the desire to eat is too strong to be denied and the dam bursts. After a binge, many revert to siding with the superego; they hate themselves for overeating. Others go numb to how emotionally and physically uncomfortable they feel. Unlike bulimics and some anorexics, people with binge-eating disorder don't have the luxury of hiding their eating disorder. They wear their illness on the outside. This creates an exorbitant amount of shame and personal pain, which makes it even harder for them to do the self-love work that is necessary for recovery.

Some of the treatment challenges with people who have binge-eating disorder are a lack of motivation due to despair about size (the fact of their weight causes them to agree with the superego) and re-luctance to exercise because it puts them in touch with their bodies or they have weight-related injuries.

A Fight to the Death

In all three ED types, frequently the ego is not developed enough to register the pain, nor is it strong enough to come forward and say, "Break it up!" to the id and superego. This means that the su-perego and id continue to fight unabated. As long as they are fight-ing, their conflict dominates the psychic stage, removing the focus from the physical and emotional consequences of the eating-dis-order behaviors. In this way, the conflict between superego and id is a tool of denial. In this battle, there is no winner. It is a fight to the death, killing the souls and sometimes the bodies of people with eating disorders. Intervention is required to break the cycle of internal violence.

How the Superego Became Aggressive and Violent

What follows is information on how the tyrannical superego devel-ops, and indications for the treatment of eating disorders.[18]

Freud teaches us that the superego forms in such a way as to ensure the survival of the ego and the individual. Why, then, would a mechanism whose purpose is to aid survival destroy the very be-ing it is supposed to protect? What went wrong? The answer lies in recent research on attachment. When Freud astutely recognized that the superego develops in such a way as to promote survival in the person's family, this was understood primarily through the

---

18 A body of data-based research on these phenomena has yet to be created. For now, the following statement by Mark Edmundson, excerpted from his book on the end of Freud's life serves best to explain how the conclusions above demonstrate scientific discovery and rigor: "Freud provides a way of looking at experience that — like Samuel Johnson's way, or Montaigne's or Emerson's — can be proved or disproved not by scientific standards, but by individuals deploying his ideas and honestly chronicling the gains and losses that follow." (Edmundson, Mark: *The Death of Sigmund Freud* (New York: Bloomsbury USA, 2007), 161.

lens of physical survival and adherence to the family's moral code. While researching attachment in children after World War II, however, John Bowlby and Mary Ainsworth discovered that it is not just physical survival or moral approval that a child seeks, but a secure emotional bond with a parent. The child needs a safe attachment, meaning the consistent presence of and reliable connection with a caregiver.

Building on the research begun by Bowlby, Sue Johnson, Ph.D., developed a theory of adult love based on her findings that grownups have the same attachment needs as children. This expanded our understanding of attachment as essential to all humans. Johnson writes, "The need for secure emotional connection with a few key others is considered to be hard-wired by evolution,"[19] and "…isolation, separation, or disconnection from an attachment figure is inherently traumatizing."[20]

The word "traumatizing" indicates that a break in connection is not simply unpleasant or irritating, but on par with serious physical injury. It is both excruciating and threatening to the core. The extra-large, tyrannical superego that drives eating-disorder behaviors can therefore be seen as an all-out attempt in the psyche to change the person into someone that the caregiver won't leave. The severe isolation and failure described earlier is the felt sense of being out-of-touch with a caregiver or attachment figure.

Our physical world is not perfect, and neither is any parent. Breaks in the connection with a caregiver are inevitable. But when the caregiver is chronically unavailable and the breaks are repeated and/or severe, the child develops a character structure around the trauma. That structure is the "unhealthy psyche" of the person with an eating disorder, described earlier. It is the inner landscape that features the huge superego, the depleted ego, and the id suffering from various degrees of banishment. This inner landscape is the basis for the

---

19 Johnson, Susan M. and Valerie E. Whiffen, *Attachment Theory: A Guide for Couple Therapy* (New York: Guilford Press, 2003), 107.

20 Ibid, 105.

eating-disorder behaviors, which not only mirror, but also reinforce the ego, superego, and id in their malformation.

Many times, the person with the eating disorder will be seen as the cause of family problems and becomes the "identified patient." While families and loved ones experience tremendous pain as a result of the eating disorder, it is not accurate to hold the person with the eating disorder responsible for the family's pain. The eating disorder is the result of dysfunction in the family system; it is not the cause. A caregiver may be unavailable for various reasons, including but not limited to:

- Physical illness or death
- Substance abuse
- Mental illness
- Physical, sexual, or emotional abuse
- Narcissism that makes the caregiver appear functional to the public but which, at home, does not allow the caregiver to see or relate to the child as she is
- A parent's depression, fear of abandonment, or anger which dominates the family (and for which the child may absorb responsibility)
- Any relationship in which the child must take care of the parent
- Workaholism
- Oppression from the world at large that weighs on the parent, such as the effects of racism, war, or natural disasters
- A preoccupation or obsession with something (such as a job or relationship) that takes the caregiver away from the child emotionally or physically

Again, this is not to set up a standard of perfection for parents, nor to place blame. No parent can be present and available all the time. The clinician must strike a balance that includes finding out what happened and supporting the client to grieve about it, without giving the client license to identify as a victim. This list above is offered to assist you in looking for emotional patterns in the family and/or social system that may be contributing to the client's enlarged superego and subsequently, the eating disorder. The goal is to find the emotional root of the problem and address it, while working to contain the ED behaviors themselves.

> The clinician must strike a balance that includes finding out what happened and supporting the client to grieve about it, without giving the client license to identify as a victim.

An additional factor that contributes to the formation of the unhealthy psyche (defined here as when the superego and id are in conflict and their conflict dominates) has to do with early attachment. Recent interpretations of classic attachment research reveals that one of the key functions of the attachment figure is to help the infant process feelings.[21] Emotions are overwhelming to an infant. He or she looks to the caregiver — quite literally, by looking for reactions in the face and body — to receive and re-process emotions, then reflect them back in a way the child can handle. When sad, an infant experiences herself as overwhelmed and overtaken by the sadness. The healthy (securely attached) mother or father may register the sadness with her own reaction, then put the sadness in a larger context. For instance, upon seeing her child cry, the mother may wrinkle her eyes in concern, say "Aww," and then, "We waited too long and now you got hungry." Registering the sadness but still letting the child know that the situation can be handled, the mother then may soothe the child — but with an acceptance that the child did, in fact, feel sad. The child then gets to experience, through the reflection by the mother, the original sadness, but in a form that is no longer overwhelming. This demonstrates to

---

21 Wallin, David, *Attachment in Psychotherapy* (New York: Guilford Press, 2007), 145.

the child that she does not need to fear her own emotions, that her mother is not afraid of them, and that their connection is still solid, even though there was a lot of emotion happening. She therefore does not learn to reject feelings, or herself for having them.

Alternatively, the caregiver may not be able to re-process the emotions and mirror them back to the child. The child can elicit a parent's own sadness and the parent herself may be overwhelmed by it. In this instance, instead of emotions being reflected back in a manageable state, there is even more unmanageability in the child's experience. In this situation, the child learns early that it is dangerous to elicit a negative reaction in the caregiver. Two things then result: (1) the emotions remain overwhelming and (2) the child begins to reject herself for having them as she sees they create distance from or rejection by the caregiver. This sets the stage for the id to develop in such a way as to be scary and overwhelming, like the emotions themselves. The uncontrollable emotions, through the overwhelming id, then contribute to being "out of control" with overeating or restricting.

It is worth noting that if the caregiver cannot re-process a child's emotions, this is likely an indication that her caregivers did not do so for her. Therefore, her id and superego would have also had to develop in a vacuum, without the loving containment they needed. In this sense the parent's inability to provide what the child needs is not something for which to blame the parent, but rather an entry in a tragic timeline that gets passed down from generation to generation.

When working with an eating-disordered client, it is key to find that moment when she got the message that she should repress the id, and when she learned to reject herself for having needs and emotions. This moment may be traced back to a discrete point in time, but sometimes you need only to search for a pattern, as the inspiration for the repression is often repeated in current communications with the parents, loved ones, and with the therapist. Psychotherapy provides the context for re-experiencing the emotions so that they become integrated in the person's experience and psyche.

As the person gets older, the uncontained id develops along with its counterpart: a voluminous and punitive superego. When the child's emotions are met with either the parent's overwhelming emotions or by a parent who wants to fix the child or take her pain away, the child gets the message that the emotional part of herself is unacceptable. Since those emotions remain uncontained and they loom large in her experience, the child may then perceive them to be herself. A kind of core identity develops, leading the child to conclude at some level, "This mess of emotions is who I am and who I am is unacceptable." The large, uncontained superego that develops along with the large, uncontained emotions (and id) then becomes the agent of unacceptability and rejection, showing up in the person with an eating disorder as the voice that says, "You are disgusting and you don't deserve to eat."

The enlarged superego provides three primary benefits. The first is that it takes a person out of the despair and abject terror of losing the connection with the attachment figure and dealing with the overwhelming emotions. It provides a sense of hope. The thinking goes, "If I change myself (by losing weight, not being needy, etc.), then the person will love me and not leave me. Also, if I can contain my id, then I won't trigger negative emotions in my parent." The second "benefit" is a sense of punishment that feels just and right. The unconscious logic is, "I failed at my job of bringing the caregiver toward me or sparing her pain, so I deserve to be punished." The third "benefit" of an enlarged superego is that it gives the person an internalized version of the rejecting caregiver, so he does not experience the profound sense of aloneness that lies beneath — because anything, even abuse, is perceived to be preferable to isolation (as the research on attachment corroborates).

Narcissism: The Other Killer

The violence of narcissism is sometimes overlooked and misunderstood. Since it is such a big factor in eating-disorder formation, it deserves special attention in eating-disorder treatment. When an emotional exchange happens in such a way that a parent or caregiver's feelings overwhelm the interaction, the child then becomes a projection of those feelings rather than a full human in connection with the caregiver. Psychologically speaking, the child is not in the relationship at that moment. This break in connection feels devastating to a child and is similar to what an adult experiences when having a bad fight with a loved one. The loss of the relationship then sets off a cascade of events including changes in body and brain chemistry.[22] When the connection is broken repeatedly, a person's sense of self develops in response to the physiological and neurological reactions, creating the characterological foundation for an eating disorder. In this sense, a home with no physical or sexual violence can be violent nonetheless. Your ability to search for chronic breaks in connection and your understanding of attachment will help the client stop abusing herself and turn toward what she really needs. The importance of this cannot be overemphasized, as women and men who come from families where there is no physical violence still experience a threat to their lives, first from the insecure attachments in their families, and then from the eating disorder itself. They merit the same sympathy and concern we accord the people from physically and sexually abusive homes.

External Factors

In addition to the elements already described, it is well known that external factors contribute to the occurrence of eating disorders. A

---

22 Ibid., p. 19.

Harvard researcher demonstrated that the incidence of eating disorders rose in Fiji when television was introduced.[23] The onslaught of media images in the U.S. (reported as 247 commercial messages per day on the *Consumer Reports* website in 2002) created the nearly impossible standard by which women and men measure themselves. Researchers at The Children's Hospital of Philadelphia have found a genetic link to anorexia, indicating that biology also plays a role.[24] Peer pressure and bullying have been linked to eating disorders in a study by *Beat*, the leading research and resource group on eating disorders in England. External factors such as these are just the seeds of eating disorders, however. They can only germinate and grow in a family system that supports them.

Toward Recovery
Pervasive and life-threatening as they are, full recovery from eating disorders is possible through a process of repairing internal and external boundaries and creating healthy cognitive, emotional, and physical processes to replace the unhealthy ones. The attachment wounds that give rise to the eating disorder can be healed through reducing the dominance of the superego, reintegrating the id, reflecting on life events in an emotionally engaged yet objective manner, and improving relationship connections. The next chapter describes the relationship between superego and id, with its resulting eating behaviors, in each of type of eating disorder.

---

23   Becker AE, Burwell RA, Gilman SE, Herzog DB, Hamburg P. Eating behaviours and attitudes following prolonged television exposure among ethnic Fijian adolescent girls. *The British Journal of Psychiatry.* 2002;180:509-14.

24   Source: http://www.anad.org/news/gene-links-to-anorexia-found-by-researchers-at-the-childrens-hospital-of-philadelphia/ Accessed December 11, 2010.

CHAPTER 4

Mapping the Landscape: The Eating Disorder Cycles

One way of understanding an eating disorder is to look at it as a series of thoughts, feelings and behaviors that build on each other, creating a cycle. As mentioned earlier, although the thoughts, feelings and behaviors can seem bizarre to outsiders, they make sense in the context of the emotional landscape of the eating disorder.

The primary goal in treatment is to help the person achieve an appropriate balance between the superego and id, resulting in the development of an ego that has the capacity for self-love and self-regulation (especially the regulation of eating patterns). To accomplish this, the client must reduce the power of her superego and reintegrate the needs and energy of her id into consciousness. In this process, the conflict between the id and the superego de-escalates. Feelings and urges that were once banished become acceptable, empowering the ego and allowing the client to feel worthy of nourishment. This reintegration takes place when the eating-disorder cycle is interrupted through the treatment tools and interventions you provide in session and which you give the client for use outside of session. Understanding the cycle that operates in your client will help you find the best ways to interrupt it.

> Understanding the eating disorder cycle as it operates in your client will help you find the best ways to intervene.

The cycles create their own momentum and strengthen the eating disorder on all fronts — physical, emotional and cognitive. There is no discrete beginning; each step leads to the other. At the same time, the inner critic is foundational: It is where the person starts out and where she returns in the course of her thoughts, behaviors, feelings and coming home to a sense of self.

Below you will find a delineation of how thoughts, feelings, and actions create a chain of behaviors in each of the main eating-disorder types: Anorexia Nervosa – Restricting Type, Anorexia Nervosa – Binge-Eating/Purging Type, Bulimia Nervosa, and Compulsive Overeating.[25] The reader will benefit from studying all of the cycles since clients with one disorder often relate to aspects of the others. People with Eating Disorder Not Otherwise Specified (Compulsive Overeating and Binge-Eating included) have cycles that include aspects from the other eating-disorder types, but do not meet the criteria for any single type. For them and for all your clients, it is useful to record the steps of the cycle to determine the thoughts, behaviors and feelings unique to that person's illness. (This intervention is further described in Chapter 5.) Please note that the steps in each cycle do not necessarily show up in clients in this exact order; instead, the descriptions illustrate general, underlying patterns. Note also the relationship between id, superego and ego in each cycle, and the resulting eating behaviors.

---

25 Although it is not an official diagnosis in the *DSM-IV*, the authors have included a diagram delineating the Compulsive Overeating cycle because of its prevalence in the clinical population. For the purposes of this manual, "Compulsive Overeating" includes both binge-eating and habitual overeating. Please note that what we are calling Compulsive Overeating is coded as Eating Disorder Not Otherwise Specified in the *DSM-IV*.

The conflict between superego and id and the subsequent disempowerment of the ego is the psychological hallmark of eating disorders. What differs is not this central conflict, but how the conflict manifests in thoughts, feelings and behaviors of each type.

Anorexia Nervosa – Restricting Type

Phase I: Establishment

- **Thoughts**
  The **superego rules with attacks and criticism** showing up in vicious self-judgments such as "I am fat; I am disgusting; I am worthless."
- **Feelings**
  These thoughts produce some combination of **anxiety, anguish**, and a **compulsion to appease the superego** in hope of alleviating the attacks. This compulsion often manifests as a commitment to work hard and "be better."
- **Behaviors**
  Seeking to be "good," the **client restricts or diets**, perhaps avoiding taboo foods and exercising excessively.

Phase II: Escalation

The triumph of denying human needs and appeasing the ever-louder superego serves not to reduce it, but to strengthen its hold. The person is not aware of the danger, however. Thinking she is on the right track because she is able to do its bidding, she goes further into eating-disorder behaviors. Changes in brain chemistry due to semi-starvation entrench the cycle, as they prevent clear thinking and choices.

- **Thoughts**
  The **superego praises or rewards obedience with silence.**[26] Meanwhile the vise-grip of the superego tightens underneath the apparent calm.
- **Feelings**
  The physical and emotional deprivation she experiences as a result of her restricting, exercise, and other anorexic behaviors provides an energizing "high,"[27] along with a **sense of accomplishment and power.** This inspires her to further alignment/identification with the superego and motivates her to continue being "good."
- **Behaviors**
  Restricting and exercise increase.

Phase III: Dominance

Thoughts, feelings and behaviors snowball, compacting each other. The ability to achieve new levels of caloric restriction, more hours of exercise and greater denial of natural human needs provides a sense of power and approval, which stands in for the much-yearned-for sense of being loved and lovable. Unlike the other cycles, which entail a face-off with the id, the cycle in Anorexia Nervosa – Restricting Type is characterized by increasing intimacy and identification with the superego. The id-superego conflict is "resolved" through full banishment of the id to the unconscious.

- **Feelings**
  The client feels **energized and motivated** by meeting the superego's ever-toughening standards.
- **Behaviors**
  She **restricts and over-exercises with increasing severity,** perhaps adding other forms of self-harm and/or self-denial.

---

26 The phrases in bold text appear in the visual diagram for that cycle.

27 Clients report the experience of a "high" from anorexic behaviors. Whether there is an addictive relationship to chemicals released as a result of restricting (such as adrenaline and dopamine) is yet to be corroborated by the medical community.

- **Thoughts**
  The client **renews her commitment to align with the superego**. The domineering superego becomes the main source of authority.

The growing alignment with the superego causes the cycle to repeat.

> Anorexia, and eating disorders in general, can be seen as a slow suicide. Freud's writing on suicide, described in *The Death of Sigmund Freud*, corroborates this view: "Freud suggests that the main cause of suicide is an imbalance in the psyche. The over-I [Edmundson's translation of "superego" from the German] has become too strong at the expense of the poor, depleted ego. The internal agent of authority rails at the self for its manifold inadequacies. But only when the ego is weak and unable to defend itself does it surrender to the over-I and do away with itself." (Edmundson, Mark, *The Death of Sigmund Freud*, p. 86.)

Summary

Though in some ways complex (as described above), the AN – Restricting Type cycle can be distilled into a simple relationship: the client's submission to the superego and its takeover of the psyche. Because the conflict between superego and id is quelled due to the triumph of the superego, clients with this eating disorder present as if nothing is wrong because to them, nothing is — as long as they obey the eating disorder voice (or superego). The client may develop a detached disposition or a servile affect in response to the superego's dominance. This can make the person appear "together" despite the true disaster that is taking place. Note that the conflict between id and superego is not absent; it is merely repressed. As the eating disorder progresses, the superego takes over more and more functions in the psyche (both ego and id), replacing regular human emotions such as sadness and tenderness (especially toward herself) with rejection and judgment. The person's ego is narrow and weak, which influences the body image, i.e., the self should ideally be thin, taking up no space.

Diagram 3a

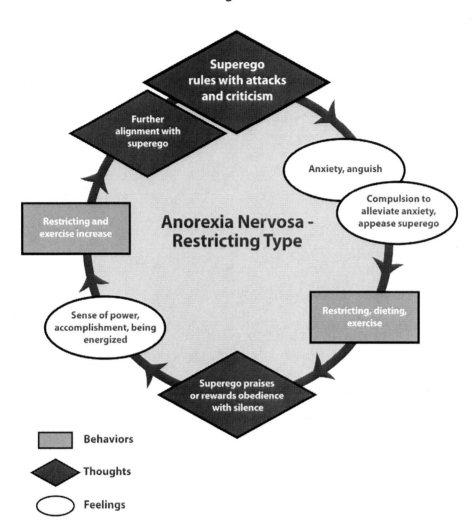

Anorexia Nervosa - Restricting Type

- Superego rules with attacks and criticism
- Further alignment with superego
- Restricting and exercise increase
- Anxiety, anguish
- Compulsion to alleviate anxiety, appease superego
- Sense of power, accomplishment, being energized
- Restricting, dieting, exercise
- Superego praises or rewards obedience with silence

Behaviors
Thoughts
Feelings

Anorexia Nervosa – Binge-Eating/Purging Type

The cycles of AN – Binge-Eating/Purging Type and AN – Restricting Type resemble each other with one major difference: People with the Binge-Eating/Purging subtype have episodes in which the id takes over for a time and they eat. Despite this resurgence, ultimately, the client with AN – Binge-Eating/Purging type "succeeds" at banishing the id as does the client with AN – Restricting Type. Most of the physical and psychological results are therefore the same, e.g. severe weight loss, refusal to maintain a minimally normal weight, and identification with the superego. Note that clients who purge from eating normal amounts (not bingeing) are also given this diagnosis. They perceive the mere act of eating as an unacceptable resurgence of the id. Accordingly, it requires compensatory behaviors in their eyes.

Phase I: Establishment

> **Thoughts** The **superego rules with attacks and criticism** showing up in vicious self-judgments such as "I am fat; I am disgusting; I am worthless."

- **Feelings**
  These thoughts produce some combination of **anxiety, anguish**, and a **compulsion to appease the superego** in hope of alleviating the attacks. This compulsion often manifests as a commitment to work harder and "be better."
- **Behaviors**
  Seeking to be "good," the **client restricts or diets**, perhaps avoiding taboo foods and exercising excessively.
- **Feelings**
  As a result of restricting, the **client feels empty and numb.**

Feeling empty and numb presents a choice for the person with this diagnosis: The client may feel powerful and energized as a result of being empty and numb, or she may feel emotionally and physically deprived. Feeling powerful motivates her to repeat the cycle above;

feeling deprived causes her to go into the next phase of the cycle, described below.

Phase II: Anorexic Rebellion

As a result of the restricting and dieting, the person with AN – Binge-Eating/Purging Type will, at some point, respond to the hunger by feeling deprived and having a resurgence of the id called an Anorexic Rebellion. This sets in motion an additional set of thoughts, behaviors and feelings in the cycle.

- **Feelings**
  Whereas at other times it gave her a high and a boost of energy, this time **the restricting leaves her feeling physically and emotionally deprived.**
- **Behaviors**
  Client eats or binges.
- **Feelings**
  The eating or binge provides a momentary sense of **relief.**
- **Thoughts**
  After the brief reprieve, **vitriolic self-criticism** roars in. Having eaten is seen as a punishment for disobeying the superego. The intensity of the attacks may or may not correspond to the amount of food eaten.[28]
- **Feelings**
  The client may have intense feelings of **failure, self-hatred and despair** along with a **compulsion to alleviate these feelings.**
- **Behaviors**
  Client compensates by **purging, exercising excessively, taking laxatives, etc.**
- **Feelings**

---

28 Some clients are self-critical for eating a little food, or eating certain foods; others are critical for eating any food at all. Still other clients only get the severe self-punishment if they binge.

Having renewed her commitment to the superego, the client experiences **relief.**

- **Behaviors**
  Restricting and exercise increase.

Phase III: Dominance

At this stage, the person with AN – Binge-Eating/Purging Type considers herself "back on track" and the rest of the ED cycle resembles that of AN – Restricting Type.

- **Feelings**
  The client feels **energized and motivated** by meeting the superego's ever-toughening standards.
- **Behaviors**
  She **restricts and over-exercises with increasing severity,** perhaps adding other forms of self-harm and/or self-denial.
- **Thoughts**
  The client **renews her commitment to align with the superego**. The domineering superego becomes the main source of authority.

Summary

The relationship between the superego and id is more complex in AN Binge-Eating/Purging Type but, ultimately, the takeover by the superego is the same in both types of anorexia. Her identification with the inner critic creates the sense that everything is OK (as long as she succeeds in doing its bidding), which can be lethal as her health crumbles but she does not see a problem. The ability to achieve new levels of caloric restriction, more hours of exercise and greater denial of natural human needs provides a sense of power and approval, which approximates the much yearned-for sense of being loved and lovable.

Diagram 3b

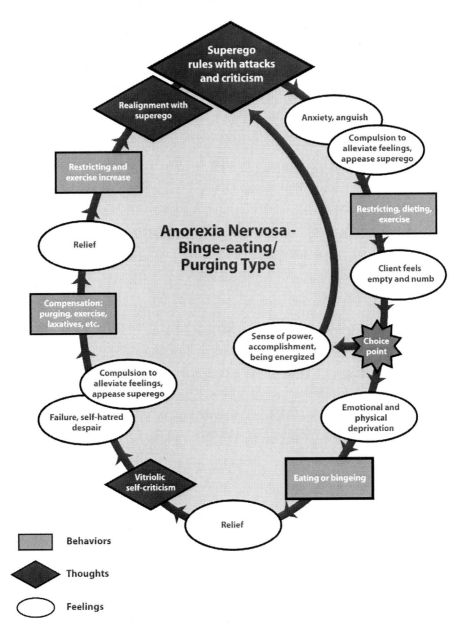

Bulimia Nervosa

The cycle of Bulimia Nervosa resembles that of Anorexia Nervosa – Binge-Eating/Purging Type with the difference that in AN, complete identification with the superego takes place, while bulimics do not "succeed" in fully repressing the id. Though they hate themselves for this perceived failure, in many cases the accessibility of the id can be harnessed to inspire the person with bulimia to live and recover.

Phase I: Establishment

- **Thoughts**
  The **superego rules with attacks and criticism** showing up in vicious self-judgments such as "I am fat; I am disgusting; I am worthless."
- **Feelings**
  These thoughts produce some combination of **anxiety, anguish**, and a **compulsion to appease the superego** in hope of alleviating the attacks. This compulsion often manifests as a commitment to work hard and "be better."
- **Behaviors**
  Seeking to be "good," the **client restricts or diets**, perhaps avoiding taboo foods and exercising excessively.
- **Feelings**
  The client feels physically and emotionally deprived.

Feeling physically and emotionally deprived presents a choice for the bulimic. She may feel strong enough to keep pushing herself to restrict and exercise, or she may feel too emotionally and physically deprived to continue. If she can push herself, she will repeat the cycle above. If she is unable to push herself further, she will go into the next phase of the cycle, described below.

Some bulimics stay in Phase One for days before succumbing to hunger; others sustain Phase One for a matter of hours before bingeing begins. Instead of identifying with the inner critic, as the anorexic person tends to, the bulimic may identify as its victim. This contributes to the resurgence of the id since, as the victim, the person is aware of feeling emotionally as well as physically deprived.

Phase II: Id Takeover

Although superego attacks are severe and abusive for bulimics, the bulimic tends to fear the appearance of the id much more than the superego, perceiving the id as the source of trouble. She tries to suppress the id, but the dagger-like invectives from the superego only inflame the id further until there is a hostile takeover by the id and the client binges.

- **Feelings**
  She has a compulsion to eat.
- **Behaviors**
  The client binges.[29]
- **Feelings**
  During the binge, the client experiences **relief**.[30]
- **Thoughts**
  After being temporarily subdued by eating, the client's inner critic now returns with **vitriolic criticism**.
- **Feelings**
  The client feels an intolerable sense of **failure, self-hatred and despair**.
- **Behaviors**
  The client tries to "undo" the binge by **purging, over-exercising**, or a combination of **compensatory behaviors**.

---

29 Certain clients report the experience of a runaway train or a volcano exploding. Others report a kind of eating blackout in which their normal decision-making functions are not available.

30 As a client poignantly put it, "The comfort ends as soon as you swallow."

Phase III: Clean-Slate Period

This third phase resembles that of anorexia, with the added pathos that the bulimic is convinced of her own despicability due to the binge-purge behaviors and her inability to adhere to the standards of the superego.

- **Feelings**
  Client experiences **relief** from having "redeemed herself" and may feel optimistic due to the prospect of a clean slate.
- **Thoughts**
  Her **commitment to align with the superego renewed**, the superego's rule is now reinstated.

Shame and the compulsion to do the behaviors, then hide them, can isolate the bulimic from others. Depression may occur as a result of this or, if it was present at the onset of the disease, it intensifies.

Summary

If Bulimia Nervosa were a play, the central dramatic conflict would be the battle for ascendancy between the superego and id. But the play would be a tragedy because when either one wins, the person herself inevitably loses. The victim is the ego which, in the wake of this violence, has no energy left over, even for its very existence. As a result, this central conflict becomes the person's identity.

Diagram 4

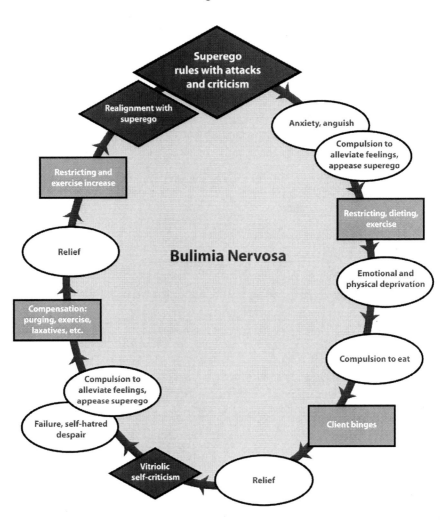

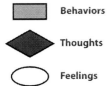 Behaviors

Thoughts

Feelings

Compulsive Overeating

In the conflict between id and superego in the compulsive overeater, the superego tries to dominate, but the id wins the battle. This is only when it comes to food, however. In other areas, the superego dominates as it does with eating disorders in general (although the id-superego relationship for compulsive overeaters can be particularly nuanced and complex). The ascendancy of the superego over the id or vice versa requires a dance of sending the unwanted part of the psyche into the unconscious. Denial is therefore an important part of the compulsive-overeating cycle.

Phase I: Tension-Building

- **Thoughts**
  The **superego rules with attacks and criticism** showing up in vicious self-judgments such as "I am fat; I am disgusting; I am worthless." (Note the similarity to anorexia and bulimia.)
- **Feelings**
  These thoughts produce some combination of **anxiety, anguish**, and a **compulsion to appease the superego** in the hope of alleviating attacks. This compulsion often manifests as a commitment to work harder and "be better."
- **Behaviors**
  Seeking to be "good," the **client restricts or diets**, perhaps avoiding certain foods.
- **Feelings**
  The client feels physically and emotionally deprived.

Like the bulimic, the compulsive overeater may identify as the victim of the inner critic. This contributes to the resurgence of the id since, as the victim, the person is aware of feeling emotionally as well and physically deprived.

Phase II: Compulsivity Period

- **Feelings**
  The client has **an irresistible urge to eat.**
- **Behaviors**
  Client binges or overeats. (Some compulsive overeaters eat an amount that is excessive but does not meet the criteria for a full binge.) Eating allows her to go into denial about her feelings.
- **Thoughts**
  The id takes over and the superego is temporarily unconscious.

Phase III: Aftermath

In Phase Three, the person stops eating because food is no longer comforting. Some clients feel physically too full to continue; others experience a profound sense of failure and despair about having overeaten. The superego will surface again in reaction to the binge. This presents a choice point for the compulsive overeater. She will either cycle back to Phase Two and begin eating again, or experience failure and despair about the situation and move into Phase Three.[31]

- **Feelings**
  Food ceases to comfort.
- **Behaviors**
  Client stops eating/bingeing.
- **Feelings**
  Client may feel a **sense of failure, self-hatred and despair** about having eaten or binged and about her overall condition.

---

31 Some clients report a simultaneous experience: As the superego is putting her down for having overeaten, she fantasizes about food as an escape from this pain.

- **Thoughts**
  The superego returns with powerful criticism. Its accusations having been "proven," the person **submits to the superego** and its rule is reinstated.

Although the compensatory behaviors that characterize bulimia and AN – Binge-Eating/Purging Type are absent, the psychological result and the client's experience is similar, e.g., the person ultimately agrees with the superego.

The compulsive overeater's dilemma is best captured in a scene from *The Little Prince* in which the prince encounters a drunkard. (Substitute "eating" for "drinking.")

"What are you doing here," he asked the drunkard...

"Drinking," replied the drunkard, with a gloomy expression.

"Why are you drinking?" the little prince asked.

"To forget," replied the drunkard.

"To forget what?" inquired the little prince, who was already feeling sorry for him.

"To forget that I'm ashamed," confessed the drunkard, hanging his head.

"What are you ashamed of?" inquired the little prince, who wanted to help.

"Of drinking!" concluded the drunkard... [From *The Little Prince* by Antoine de Saint-Exupery]

Summary

As the cycle repeats in the long term, the person feels anguish about her physical and psychological health. Unlike the bulimic, whose sense is that she is sometimes able to meet the standards of the superego, the compulsive overeater's hope for success is dim. As with bulimia, shame and the compulsion to engage in and then hide the behaviors can isolate the compulsive overeater from others. Alternatively, she may be in denial of her feelings and concerns, using the eating behaviors to drown them out. This exacerbates her physical and psychological condition.

In compulsive overeating, the superego never lets the id forget how despicable it is for winning the battle when it comes to food. The argument could be made that the availability of id energy makes this eating disorder less lethal than its cousin, anorexia. Unfortunately, the threats to physical health and the pain of the psychological conflict are comparable; the person is left suffering. The fact that the client can use her size as a confirmation of her failure entrenches her in an identity-prison where the superego supplies endless putdowns, holding the id as its victim.

Please see the Compulsive Overeating diagram, next page.

Diagram 5

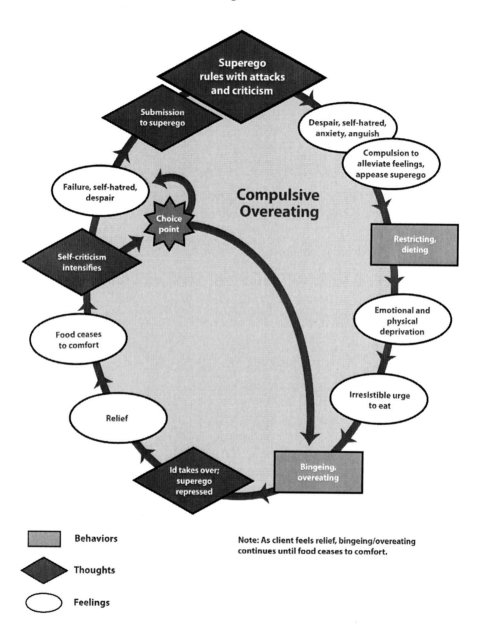

Compulsive Overeating

Superego rules with attacks and criticism

Submission to superego

Despair, self-hatred, anxiety, anguish

Compulsion to alleviate feelings, appease superego

Failure, self-hatred, despair

Choice point

Restricting, dieting

Self-criticism intensifies

Emotional and physical deprivation

Food ceases to comfort

Irresistible urge to eat

Relief

Id takes over; superego repressed

Bingeing, overeating

Behaviors

Thoughts

Feelings

Note: As client feels relief, bingeing/overeating continues until food ceases to comfort.

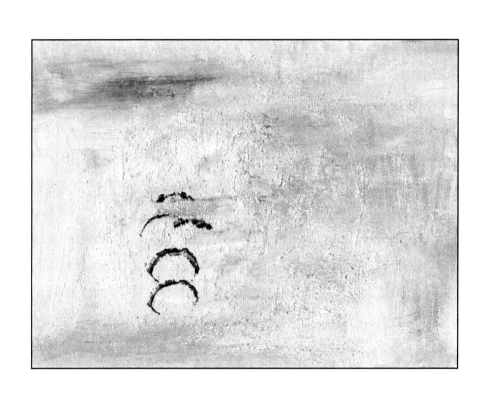

Part Three

Plate 3: *In Flight*

See my wings. Now touch them.
Feel the logic in their equation,
how they add up and matter with their
Hard bones inside
and their freedom.
My bones are from here.
I am part of this.

CHAPTER 5

Breaking the Cycle: A Treatment Philosophy and Interventions for a Clinical Setting

One of the most effective ways to treat eating disorders is to help the individual create structured time with concrete tools, so she feels contained and safe. Use of the tools decreases the pull of the cycle and reduces the impulse to fall back on the eating disorder to combat attacks from the superego. Furthermore, a primary goal in the treatment of eating disorders is to help the client develop external and internal boundaries, a crucial part of ego development. External boundaries maintain the client's safety in interpersonal relationships, allowing her to set limits with others when needed. In doing so, her id is supported and her ego strength is elevated. Internal boundaries allow her to set limits on her superego. In this way, she reduces the power of the superego when she asserts the needs of the id. By asserting her feelings (i.e., expressing them) rather than reacting to feelings (i.e., escaping into ED behaviors), she can relinquish her eating disorder and embrace self-worth. External boundary-setting happens between the client and another person, whereas internal boundary-setting happens between the client and her own superego.

Some people describe a black-and-white experience, a takeover by either id or superego when they are restricting or in the middle of a binge. Others report a more mixed experience: The superego is on their shoulder while eating, which spurs the id to eat more under pressure in a compulsion to "get it while you can"; or that when the person is restricting, the id is close, begging to be fed. The treatment interventions described in Chapter 6 differ in technique, but their common denominator is the de-escalation of the battle between the id and the superego, since the battle is what fuels the eating-disorder behaviors.

Integrating Interventions into a Treatment Plan

Eating-disorder interventions, from self-nourishment to expressing feelings and challenging obsessive thoughts, serve the larger goals of reducing the inner critic, reintegrating the id, and empowering the ego. Expanding a person's range of emotions, experiences, and thoughts increases the amount of psychic energy available, while also increasing what will be accepted as part of her central identity. The stronger ego then provides a reliable alternative to the beliefs, feelings, and behaviors of the eating disorder.

Because an ED is a takeover of the person's identity and functioning, it is important to develop a treatment plan that addresses the eating disorder on a variety of levels, from the practical and physical, to the cognitive and the emotional. Does she require extra encouragement to access her id, or does she need you to focus on boundaries, showing her how choices made out of love can be an alternative to the abusive superego? The four types of eating disorders described previously, with their varying roles of id and superego, are a guideline within which you will design a treatment plan geared to the unique needs of your client.

Many of the men and women who have eating disorders have endured emotional, physical, or sexual abuse. They have been victims of hostile takeovers by the id (in themselves or others), and are hesitant to welcome the id back into their lives. Similarly, they have not been exposed to a positive superego function of firmness; their impression is that boundary-setting is synonymous with harshness and emotional or physical violence. As an overall part of treatment, it is therefore important to help clients distinguish between appropriate and inappropriate expressions of id and superego — that either one, in its place and in the right proportion, can be a force for good.

In your treatment plan construction, use the entire team to create a holistic plan, including the professional insights and recommendations of all members: dietician, psychiatrist, medical doctor, etc. This will benefit your client and allow you to focus on your part of the whole process.

What follows is a description of concrete techniques and tools for interrupting the eating-disorder cycle. Additional treatment tools can be found on the DVD, *Erasing ED*.

The ED treatment interventions are divided into three different modalities:

- Cognitive Behavioral Interventions
- Expressive Arts and Writing Interventions
- Interpersonal Interventions

Cognitive Behavioral Interventions

Cognitive Behavioral tools provide structure and boundaries that allow the individual to reclaim power over her actions and alter the thoughts that inform her feelings and dysfunctional behaviors.

- **Stop Thought/New Choice**: When the negative and self-deprecating thought enters the psyche, "Stop" it immediately (saying "Stop!" out loud or in thought) and replace it with a positive "new choice" (a positive thought or an *action distraction*, such as making a call to a support person or checking email). The objective is to disrupt the negative thought pattern immediately and create healthy substitutions.

- **Alternative-Choice Journal**: The client writes down his *feeling* ("I feel lonely"), followed by his *action* ("I'll binge and purge"), followed by the *consequence* ("I'll end up feeling out of control"), followed by the *alternative choice* ("I'll do a support call instead and ask for help"). This tool offers a chain analysis that clarifies how the individual could choose healthy behaviors in lieu of the ED behaviors when negative impulses arise.

- **ED Cycle Diagram:** You and the client record the thoughts, feelings and behaviors of the eating disorder in a visual format using the shapes and colors of her choice. Show the sequence of events, choice points, and repetitive patterns in time. Then review the diagram with the client, agreeing on interventions that would disrupt the cycle at each juncture. This is also known as a "chain analysis." (Appendix A includes a blank cycle diagram, an alternative to the art-oriented cycle activity above.)

> The chain-analysis method helps the client connect the ED behavior with ensuing emotional duress and learn to choose healthier behaviors.

- **Positive Affirmations:** Invite the client to make a list of positive "I" statements affirming her worth that help to build ego strength and reduce the inner critic (e.g., "I am a good listener"). It is helpful to do this exercise with the client because shame can be an enormous barrier to change. For instance, the clinician can join the individual by writing three positive affirmations about her. Once client and clinician complete the affirmations, they can be read out loud in session.

- **Superego Counterattacks**: This is a method in which you show the client how to fight off the criticism of the superego. It has a series of steps described below.

Superego: Friend or Foe? Instruct the client about how the superego works. (You can use the healthy/unhealthy psyche diagrams [pp. 31, 34-35] and the ED Cycles [pp. 53, 57, 61] provided in this manual.) Plant a seed of doubt that the superego is a well-intentioned or accurate voice of authority. Next, teach the client these four steps to superego defense:

1. **Notice:** Educate the client to notice when she is under attack. Help her identify the physical signs (such as shortness of breath) and emotional signs (such as irritability or being in a bad mood).

2. **Identify**: Show the client how to investigate the specific superego attack so she can identify it. Start by asking her what it's saying. Is it "You are fat!" "You are ugly!" or "You are unlovable!"? Or is the attack nonverbal and energetic, giving the client a sense of being in the grip of a negative force?

3. **Feel**: Ask the client to experience and then describe the genuine emotion she has in response to the attack. Describing the feeling can invite "feeling the feeling" which is the therapeutic goal. If the superego is saying, "You're fat!", a retort in the same mode such as "I am not fat!" will not change the energy of the superego, nor lessen its impact. Every time the client experiences a genuine emotion in the face of an attack, however, some of the energy that has been hijacked by the superego gets reclaimed by the rest of the system (the id and ego).

4. **Disengage**: After the client has allowed her feelings without judgment, she may have an experience of compassion for herself. This compassion helps the client

see that the attack actually hurts her and that she does not deserve to be hurt. (Some clients understand right away that they do not deserve abuse. Others take longer to see this.) At this point, encourage the client to choose an action in response to the superego. Does she choose self-advocacy, in which she expresses her feelings (somatic and emotional), or does she choose self-protection, in which she fights off the superego? Another way to look at this question is: Will she be more successful in this intervention if she says "yes" to the id, or "no" to the superego?

a. **Sense In and Express Truth**: This is saying yes to the id. Especially in the beginning of treatment, people with eating disorders may not have enough id energy to fight back. These clients benefit from the simple act of claiming their id by saying exactly how they are feeling, even if it's "I feel weak and I don't know what to say." This aligns them with the plight of the id instead of the judgments of the superego.

b. **Sense In and Fight Back**: This is saying no to the superego. Take a gentle lead in showing the client how to sense her emotions. When the client gets stronger, teach her to tap into her anger and utilize angry responses to set boundaries with the superego, such as swearing at it, telling it to back off, or saying, "You have no right to talk to me that way."

Prepare Your Defense: As ammunition for the steps described above, have the client make a list of the favorite attacks by her superego and what she could say or do in response to them. Then, she can practice her defense on a physical level by drawing a picture of the superego, taping the picture up on the wall, and throwing balls of Sculpey (or something else safe) at it. Afterward, she can tear up the picture, wad it up and throw it out. (This exercise is best done in a group.)[32]

---

32 For more information on how to work on the superego with clients, go to www.sheirakahn.com

There is a paradox at the heart of superego disengagement: When a client lets herself become vulnerable, she is better equipped to combat the eating-disorder voice (or superego). Defensiveness is the inner critic's stock-in-trade, and if she engages with it on the levels of defensiveness or reason, the inner critic will always win. By allowing and then expressing emotion, on the other hand, she is introducing authentic id energy, re-allocating it from the superego back to the id, and changing the terms of the engagement. In the face of an attack, it can be counterintuitive to become vulnerable, yet it is the only way out, especially in the beginning, when anger from the id may not be available for use in defense against the superego.

- **No Self-Harm/No Suicide Contract:** If a client reports a history of self-harm or suicidal intentions, or if he is reporting these currently, have him sign a No Self-Harm and/or No Suicide Contract. The No Self-Harm Contract should include a list of behaviors to be avoided along with a description of alternative actions the client can take in place of the self-harming behaviors. The No Suicide Contract also lists phone numbers of people, hotlines, and/or agencies the person can call when he is in danger, in order of what would be done first, second, etc. Both client and therapist sign and date the contracts and take copies. Contracts should be reviewed frequently, according to the needs of the client. Many examples of these contracts are available on the Internet.
- **Binge Contract (for EDNOS) or Binge-Purge Contract (for Anorexia or Bulimia):** Ask the client how many times per week he is currently bingeing and/or purging. Next, inquire whether he is willing to reduce it by one and record that number on a tracking sheet.[33] For example, if he binges

---

33 The tracking sheet should be visible to the client — don't put the information in your progress notes where he can't see it — but it need not be signed by the client, as a formal contract may seem punitive. What we are calling a contract is

five times per week, the agreement is that he may binge up to four times per week. Work week-by-week with your client, reducing the number of binges only if the client feels ready and only after two consecutive weeks of meeting the goal.

Contracts gradually eliminate dysfunctional behaviors through creating accountability and a sense of containment. It is important to negotiate the contract with the cooperation of the client so the individual feels empowered. If the client feels that the therapist is "making the rules," then the contract and the therapist will appear just as the eating disorder does: rigid and controlling.

Removing the taboo of bingeing and putting a boundary on the behavior through the Binge-Purge Contract defuses the id/superego conflict. Subsequently, compulsivity decreases and a sense of empowerment develops over time.

- **Delay Binge-Purge:** Ask the individual to delay the ED behavior by 10–20 minutes. In that time, she must agree to engage in healthy *action distractions* (e.g., take a walk, call a support person, check email, etc.) If she still wants to binge-purge at the close of the 10–20 minutes, she can do so. Frequently, it is reported that the urge to engage in ED behaviors diminishes over the elapsed time.
- **Feelings Journal:** Keeping a regular Feelings Journal helps to document the client's recovery process and identify painful feelings directly. It builds tolerance for intimacy with self and engages the nonlinear part of the brain, increasing accessibility to the client's inner resources. This tool can also be a direct alternative to ED behaviors (i.e., "Instead of bingeing, write in Feelings Journal").

---

in fact a verbal agreement made between therapist and client that is recorded on paper by the therapist.

- **List of Rules and Rituals about Food/Exercise:** This activity illuminates historical behaviors steeped in rigid ED practices. An example of a rule might be, "I don't allow myself to eat after 4 pm"; a ritual might be, "I weigh myself before and after each meal." Seeing the list on paper creates objectivity, replacing the compulsivity with free choice.
- **Brush Teeth:** This simple act creates a physical boundary that discourages the individual from continuing to eat beyond physical hunger. Clients report that the taste of the toothpaste or mouthwash is incompatible with the desire to consume sweet or savory foods afterwards. It can also signify the end of a binge and help the client move on.
- **Beeline:** Using this tool, the individual literally "beelines," walking directly from a potentially triggering environment into a safe environment. For example, if he arrives home after a dinner with friends and fears that he will purge his meal, he agrees to beeline to his room and write in his journal, call a support person, read a book, etc.
- **Treatment Goal Record:** Write SMART treatment goals down in session weekly and have the client sign the paper. (SMART stands for: Specific, Measurable, Attainable, Realistic, and Timely.) Offer a copy to the client. Examples: Purchase a magazine that is supportive and enjoyable instead of a (triggering) fashion magazine; buy single-serving desserts instead of a full bag. Weekly SMART goals benefit the client as they make progress visible and tangible, creating account-ability and a sense of security. Even tiny goals and successes count.
- **Food, Hunger, and Satiety Log:** Working with the dietician, invite the client to record food consumption along with hunger and satiety levels in a daily log. The log illustrates patterns of restricting, bingeing, and emotional eating while providing objectivity and consciousness in the face of unconscious ED behaviors.

Food, hunger and satiety interventions create a structure for the reintegration of the id by giving the client permission to eat, while maintaining boundaries on consumption or restriction. Each time the client eats in a nourishing way, she is not only encouraging cooperation between the id and superego, she is also building an inner world that is harmonious, which strengthens the ego.

Interventions Using Expressive Arts and Writing

This treatment modality encourages insight and awareness through the use of artistic expression. Artistic skill does not play a role in this process. Writing helps the client increase intimacy with herself and allows her to see the internal dysfunction in black and white. These exercises are simple to orchestrate in session and accessible to the client outside of session. Note: Moving into a creative modality can bring in a great deal of vulnerability for the person with an eating disorder.

Making art can bring up the inner critic strongly for some people. They see the art as coming from the part of themselves they wish to quell and may be inclined to destroy what they make. You may need to offer extra support, along with a request that they not destroy their art for at least six months.

- **Three-Panel Pictures:** This technique can help the client to recognize her distorted body image. Ask the individual to draw three separate pictures: one of how others see her body; a second of how she sees her own body; and a third of her ideal body image.
- **Life With/Without ED:** Ask the individual to create one draw-ing that depicts his life with ED, and another that excludes ED.

In this way, the freedom and value of life without ED can be expressed. People in early recovery might report feelings of loss and fear about how to cope if ED is gone, since ED consumes so much time and energy.

- **Draw ED:** Direct the client to draw the eating disorder, including its color and shape, its flow of movement, and its different parts. Next, ask her to write down ED's intentions and what it says to her verbally. Encourage her to embody ED as she does this, so she can experience what ED is actually trying to do. If your client is so inclined, encourage her to use her art process to chronicle her recovery. Reviewing her art will reveal recovery insights and progress.

- **ED Timeline:** This exercise helps the client learn why and how her eating disorder developed over time. As a visual tool, it will illuminate how the events in her life shaped not only her eating disorder, but also her mental and physical health. Using a large piece of paper and multi-colored pens or pencils, create a timeline that tracks the development of the following: body-image issues, explicit eating-disorder behaviors, chemical-dependency issues (if applicable), significant life events or crises (relating to family, trauma, and/or significant relationships), mental health issues (such as depression, anxiety, etc.), and any significant physical health issues/events (surgeries or illness). Use a color key to differentiate the variables above, and be sure to include important notes beside significant dates/periods/issues that further describe the client's experience. Completion of the timeline can occur over several sessions.

- **Clothing Burial:** Ask the individual to bring in an article of clothing that is either too small, unhealthily small, or somehow connected to her self-effacing inner critic. Invite her to explore the feelings associated with the clothing, and then to destroy the clothing in session (by cutting it up with scissors, tearing it apart, marking it up with pen, etc.) The objective is to align with her recovery voice and remove power from the ED voice.

- **Body Tracing:** This activity is appropriate to do in a closed-group setting. Clients pair up and trace one another's clothed bodies on butcher paper. Clothing should be fitted to obtain a more accurate depiction of body shape and size. Clients can then begin to experience the real versus distorted images of their bodies. The clinician can also create a list of words that the individual attaches to the various parts of the body tracing, such as anger, fear, love, acceptance, sadness, shame, male, female, mother, father, etc.

> Attaching words to the body tracing allows the client to see where she holds feelings in her body. This exercise will also illustrate how she experiences her body shape in relation to the family dynamics.

The drawings will inform the dialogue in subsequent sessions. Please note it is not recommended to do this technique in an individual session. The experience of having one's peer trace her body (rather than the therapist) is safer since the power differential doesn't exist in the peer-to-peer relationship. Additionally, client-therapist boundaries are respected by not engaging in this type of physical contact.

- **Letter to Body Part/Body Part's Response:** The individual is asked to write an authentic, uncensored letter to the part of her body with which she has the most negative association. After reading this aloud in session, the client writes from the perspective of that body part. This exercise helps to externalize the inner critic and build compassion toward her body.
- **Letters to ED:** Have the client write one letter to the eating disorder near the beginning of treatment, and another near the end. The two letters are bound to be very different. In the beginning of treatment, clients may acknowledge their fear of life without ED. Others may articulate how much ED hurts and

causes suffering to the client and people around her. The second letter, written in the late stage of treatment, may acknowledge how it served her and delineate the ways in which she no longer needs it. Some people use the second letter as a formal release in which they thank, forgive, and cut ties with ED.

- **Letter to Family Member:** Many ED clients benefit from expelling hidden and/or untapped feelings through letters to family members. It is helpful to ask the client to read and discuss the letters in session. This is a place to weave in the work on setting boundaries. He can choose to send the letters later (or not) or engage in family therapy at some point.
- **Letter from the Treatment-Resistant Part:** Ask the client to write a letter to herself from the part that wants to have and keep the eating disorder. This exploration and permission for those feelings makes the resistance conscious, reducing its power.
- **Letter to Inner Child/Child's Response:** By writing to a younger part of herself, the client elicits compassion for the wounded parts, building a new and healthier internal intimacy. The Child's Response Letter allows the individual to assume the role of the inner child and experience those feelings directly. It is best to ask the client to write and then read the letters in session, where she feels contained and safe, and where the therapist can model kind parenting to the client. With that model in place, this exercise then allows the client to experience healthy self-parenting.

Many ED clients enter treatment with active aggression toward and rejection of the inner child. Doing art interventions in session allows the client to draw on the therapist as a healthy model for how to relate to this part of herself. Over time, she internalizes the model and begins to experience the kind parent as part of herself.

- **Dialogue with Inner Child**: Show the client how to speak to her inner child. Instruct her to close her eyes,[34] relax, and ask for the inner child to show herself. Guide the client through a gentle inquiry in which you find out how old the child is in her image, along with what she is doing and wearing. Then the therapist asks the client to answer as the inner child. The important questions for the clinician to ask are how the inner child is feeling and what she wants. Connecting with the inner child begins the process of creating inside the client the kind of attachment with a caregiver she wanted but was not able to have. It shifts a person out of self-hatred and into compassion. The dialogue with the inner child also serves to reintegrate the id, because the id harbors the repressed inner child.

- **ED Voice/Recovery Voice Role Play:** Conduct a dialogue between the ED Voice (or Inner Critic) and the Recovery Voice. The therapist and client assume these roles, then reverse them. As with Superego Counterattacks, healing occurs in this role play as the individual experiences his ED voice in an external manner.

- **YES/NO Boundary Role Play:** Teach the client to say "Yes" to his needs and "No" to the inappropriate needs of others, and to judgments from others, by asking him to engage in a role play in which he assumes the part of a friend or family member who is violating his boundaries. You (clinician) assume the role of the client's healthy ego. Show the client how boundary-setting is done. (See the "Boundary-Setting Skills" section under Interpersonal Interventions for more information.) Reverse these roles so the client experiences both parts.

---

34 If the client is a trauma survivor, she may opt to keep her eyes open and focus on a point on the floor or wall, as closing her eyes may be triggering.

Every time the client expresses a genuine feeling or need, energy that has been repressed by the superego is reclaimed by the id. This provides a corrective emotional experience of acceptance, in contrast to the rejection he likely experienced in his family of origin. Once accepted, the feeling is then on its way to becoming an integrated part of the self, strengthening the ego and making it more flexible.

- **Alter-Image Therapy:** This is a method that reduces body-image distortion through the use of photography and journaling. Please consult the *Erasing ED* DVD for a PDF that contains a full description of this technique. Alter-Image Therapy is also discussed in the film's "Tools for Recovery" section.

Interpersonal Interventions

Interpersonal tools require that the individual interact with others in order to reduce ED urges and behaviors. These tools are effective and quite powerful, as they engage the individual with his support network, providing a corrective emotional experience that counteracts the attachment wound. The ED then diminishes as the person becomes less isolated and more interactive with safe people.

- **Bookend Calls:** Ask the individual to call and leave a message on your confidential voicemail prior to engaging in a challenging event and directly afterwards. For example, if the client is anxious about having dinner alone, ask her to call and leave you a message prior to dinner, stating how she feels and what she plans to do to care for herself during the meal (e.g., listen to music, sit at the table and not at the TV, etc.) She then leaves another message after the meal, stating how she feels and what she plans to do to care for herself (e.g., leave the kitchen and read a book, contact a friend, etc.).

If the client begins to form an unhealthy reliance on you, marked by a lack of boundaries (e.g., long and uncontained voice messages, or frequent voice messages that surpass your agreement to two calls per Bookend intervention), talk with her about this immediately. This is an indication that she is feeling out of control and in need of more support such as an ED process group, additional therapy sessions, and safe contact with family and friends.

- **Boundary-Setting Skills:** This is a Psychology Education Intervention in which you show the client how to set boundaries in personal relationships. Give the client actual language to use when setting boundaries. Describe how boundary-setting involves saying no to unwanted intrusions, and saying yes to her own feelings, needs, and wants. Distinguish between the harsh commands of the superego and providing loving limits.[35] Teach the client the difference between telling someone else what to do — which is not truly setting a boundary — and telling someone what she will do in the face of the other's unwanted behavior. For example, "Don't talk to me that way," is not setting a boundary; it is issuing a command. "If you continue to talk to me that way, I will leave the room," is a boundary because it demonstrates precisely where the individual stands.

Boundaries sound logical and sensible to clients, but may be difficult to implement. A common fear is that if she stands up for herself, she will be abandoned. Reinforce the client's alternatives for personal support if the person with whom she is setting boundaries cannot deal with the client's autonomy.

---

35 "Loving Limits" is a phrase coined by Marsea Marcus and Andrea Wachter in the *Don't Diet/Live-It* workbook. Loving Limits are boundaries given with compassion. They provide containment; they are realistic without the harshness and rigidity of the unhealthy superego. When a client provides Loving Limits for herself, she is being the kind parent she sorely needs.

- **Safe Relationships**: Encourage the client to make connections with emotionally reliable people using boundary-setting skills. In the beginning, this is likely to be a mix of professionals and some recovery-oriented peers such as a therapist, teacher, sponsor, and friends. Then, when the client and her family members have learned better boundaries, repair and reconnect family relationships if possible. This gives the client a place to go when she feels the isolation and despair of the attachment wound that underlies her ED. Over time, reliable relationships obviate the need for the eating disorder, as the person is no longer alone and therefore doesn't need to punish herself anymore for failing to bring her caregivers closer.

Setting boundaries, creating safe relationships, and developing a healthy ego are processes that occur together and strengthen each other.

- **Peer Support Calls:** Once the client distinguishes between safe and unsafe relationships, she can contact support people when challenging feelings begin to arise, after an ED behavior occurs, or at any time support is needed.
- **Medical Self-Care**: Encourage the client to care for all physical ailments with a healthcare professional who understands eating disorders. As long as the M.D. is aware of the extreme emotional vulnerability of the eating-disorder patient, medical visits can be a way for the client to experience genuine support and care. If the doctor is judgmental or dismissive, medical visits will likely trigger the eating disorder.
- **Faith:** Support your client to develop trust in a set of healthy friends, nature, love, a spiritual group, art, or whatever works for her. The experience of faith — in anything — is an antidote to the grim, collapsed worldview of the eating disorder. As she

begins to realize that she is part of a larger world that is positive and vital, her self-worth will increase.

> Faith and optimism eventually replace the eating disorder as the voice of authority.

The Chart of Interventions on the following pages illustrates how the various tools interrupt the eating disorder.

Chart of Interventions (Part One)

Cognitive Behavioral Interventions

Tools and Interventions	Reduces superego	Integrates id	Expands ego	Raises self-esteem	Replaces ED behaviors	Supplants ED worldview	Transforms distorted body image	Increases self-care	Builds awareness of ED cognitions and behaviors	Strengthens boundaries
Stop Thought/New Choice	•		•						•	•
Alternative Choice Journal		•	•		•				•	
List of Positive Affirmations	•	•	•	•		•	•		•	
Superego Counterattacks	•	•	•	•	•	•	•	•	•	•
No Self-Harm/No Suicide Contract			•					•	•	•
Binge or Binge-Purge Contract	•	•			•					•
Delay Binge-Purge					•			•	•	•
Feelings Journal		•	•	•	•			•		
List of Rules and Rituals About Food/Exercise									•	
Brush teeth					•			•	•	
Beeline					•			•	•	•
Treatment Goal Record			•	•				•		
Food, Hunger, and Satiety Log	•	•	•					•	•	•

Chart of Interventions (Part Two)

Expressive Arts and Writing Interventions

Tools and Interventions	Reduces superego	Integrates id	Expands ego	Raises self-esteem	Replaces ED behaviors	Supplants ED worldview	Transforms distorted body image	Increases self-care	Builds awareness of ED cognitions and behaviors	Strengthens boundaries
Three-panel Pictures	•			•		•	•		•	
Life With/Without ED			•	•		•			•	
Draw ED	•	•	•						•	
ED Timeline						•			•	
Clothing Burial	•	•	•		•		•		•	
Body Tracing	•						•		•	
Letter to Body Part/Response	•	•	•	•			•		•	
Letters to ED	•	•	•			•				•
Letter to Family Member	•	•	•			•		•		•
Letter from Treatment-Resistant Part		•	•		•				•	
Letter to Inner Child/Response	•	•	•	•				•	•	
Dialogue with Inner Child	•	•	•	•		•		•	•	
ED Voice/Recovery Voice/Role Play	•	•	•	•					•	•
Yes/No Boundary Role Play	•	•	•					•		•
Alter-Image Therapy (see film DVD)						•	•		•	

Chart of Interventions (Part Three)

Interpersonal Interventions

Tools and Interventions	Reduces superego	Integrates id	Expands ego	Raises self-esteem	Replaces ED behaviors	Supplants ED worldview	Transforms distorted body image	Increases self-care	Builds awareness of ED cognitions and behaviors	Strengthens boundaries
Bookend Calls	•	•	•	•	•	•		•	•	
Boundary-Setting Skills	•	•	•	•	•	•		•		•
Safe Relationships	•	•	•	•	•	•		•	•	
Peer Support Calls	•	•	•	•	•	•		•	•	•
Medical Self-care	•	•		•	•	•		•		
Faith	•		•	•		•				

CHAPTER 6

Tipping the Scale: Transcribed Hypothetical Session *with Commentary*

Treatment Plan Sample:

This is an example of how to implement a treatment plan with an eating-disordered client. It shows you what to treat and in what order. It also highlights the complexity of people with these diagnoses, who commonly have co-occurring core issues — issues that have been long-standing in the person's history and create significant impairment in functioning. Core issues commonly include (but are not limited to): substance abuse, depression, anxiety, Post-Traumatic Stress Disorder (PTSD), sexual-orientation issues, and sex and love addiction. Navigating ED treatment when there are co-occurring issues can be complex, so learning to assess which issues directly impact the ED and when to address them is essential.

Name: Gretchen
Age: 24
Gender: Female

Race: Caucasian
Sexual Orientation: Heterosexual
Occupation: Full-time student; part-time food server at café
Diagnosis: Bulimia Nervosa, 307.51
                         Dysthymic Disorder, 300.4

Over the course of a few sessions, through the process of conducting your comprehensive eating-disorder assessment, Gretchen reveals the following:

- **Presenting Problem**
  Client reports that her eating disorder is "out of control." She's experiencing anxiety with respect to her relationship with her boyfriend: "I don't want my boyfriend to know about my eating disorder because I'm afraid he'll leave me or get mad at me for having it. We're about to move in together and it's been pretty easy to hide it from him up to this point. I feel like I lead two separate lives: one he knows about, and the other, my eating disorder, that nobody knows about. I feel bad and guilty about this."

- **Mental and Medical Status**
  Client is oriented x 3 and reports no suicidal ideation or history of suicide attempts. Client reports superficial cutting on her arms in high school for one year "…when my eating disorder felt really out of control." She has no current impulses to cut and has had no self-harming behaviors since then (other than the eating disorder). Her mood is slightly depressed, although her affect is fairly bright. She weighs 135 pounds and is 5'5" tall. There has been no prior treatment for her eating disorder or any other psychological issues.

- **Eating-Disorder Onset and Current Behaviors**
  Bulimia onset was "…about six years ago. I only binged and purged once a week for the first 2–3 years and it would come

and go during that time. It was bad for one year in high school (1–2X daily). I don't know why it began; maybe because I always felt fat and wanted to be thin. I've always hated my fatso body since I was about 9 years old." Currently, client binges and purges twice daily, four days a week. She reports that she does not binge and purge the remaining three days "…because I'm with my boyfriend and I don't do my eating disorder around him." Restricting occurs daily. A typical day of eating is: one apple for breakfast; one garden salad (no dressing) and one slice of plain bread for lunch; one roasted chicken breast with a baked potato (low-fat sour cream on top), a serving of broccoli and a dinner roll (with a pat of butter), and a side salad with low-cal dressing. Although dinner is appropriate, client then binges on two boxes of cookies. Exercise is "…nonexistent because I feel too fat, but I used to run about an hour every day a couple of years ago." Client engages in excessive use of the scale, weighing herself each night.

- **Abuse History**
  Client denies sexual, emotional, or physical abuse. Client's report of family dynamics suggests emotional abuse and neglect, however. (For more information, please see "Narcissism, The Other Killer," p. 44.)

- **Support Network**
  Client has a closed family system. She is moderately close with her father and fairly distant from her mother (intact marriage) and older sister. Mother is a compulsive overeater. "She never talks about feelings; she just eats all the time and then eventually blows up and yells at everyone. My dad is really sweet, but he's afraid of getting my mom mad so he's really quiet; sometimes I feel like he needs me to protect him. We all walk on eggshells around my mom." Mother's anger and volatility made her unavailable to Gretchen.

- **Substance-Abuse Issues**
  Client reports that she "feels close" with her boyfriend and friends. Much of their socializing revolves around drinking over the weekend. When asked explicitly, Gretchen reveals that she drinks 7–8 cocktails or beers each weekend night. "I started drinking like this about a year ago, when I got serious with my boyfriend. We've been together about two years. All my friends drink like this. I only do it on the weekends so I don't think it's a problem."

Clinician's Assessment

From Gretchen's report, it is probable that she learned to fear and reject her emotions because of her mother's reactivity to them. In addition, Gretchen may have repressed her emotions and needs so she could protect her father. If Gretchen's mother repeatedly reacted to dynamics in the family (or in Gretchen) in such a way that there was a chronic break in the connection with her daughter, two aspects of Gretchen's pathology could result: (1) low self-esteem and (2) an unmet desire and fear of being close to others. This, in combination with the responsibility of taking care of her dad, probably overwhelmed her psyche, contributing to the anxiety and depression. To manage these emotions and the sheer pain of the conflicting feelings of wanting, yet fearing, closeness with others, Gretchen has turned to both eating-disorder and substance-abuse behaviors.

Treatment Plan: What to Treat First and How to Go About It

Three phases of treatment will be required to assist the client in achieving health and an ability to function well. The three phases are (1) Secure Client's Safety, (2) Manage Crisis and Core Issues, and (3) Treat ED Behaviors Directly.

Phase 1: Secure Client's Safety

- **Self Harm**
  As a result of your assessment, you ascertain that Gretchen is not at risk for suicide. She has a history of cutting that correlates to an increase in eating-disorder symptoms, however. Have her sign a **No Self-Harm Contract** and discuss her ability to ask for support, should the impulse to cut arise. As she uncovers the underlying issues in treatment, the urge to harm herself may intensify; she might turn to the "benefits" she receives from cutting, for example, when she no longer receives benefits from her ED behaviors. Additionally, she reports that she's asymptomatic when she's with her boyfriend, but she's about to move in with him and cutting might become attractive if she feels internal pressure to refrain from ED behaviors in his presence.

Cutting provides two types of secondary gain: (1) reprieve from emotional burden as the dissociative behavior allows the client to detach and escape, or (2) connection to her feelings as the pain from the wound *cuts* through the numbness and dissociation and enables her to feel emotional pain. In the first example, there is a momentary departure from the superego as the client separates from her emotional and physical body. This can be attractive to the client and encourage cutting behaviors. In the second example, the superego continues to attack in response to the return of her feelings.

- **Stabilize Mood**
  Gretchen reports clinical levels of anxiety and depression, so she should have a psychiatric evaluation. If she needs medication or other psychiatric care, the psychiatrist becomes, ideally, a valuable consulting member of the treatment team. As the clinician, use your judgment, including the client's

five-axis diagnosis, about whether a psychiatric evaluation is needed.

- **Monitor Physical Health**
  Since Gretchen is still having ED symptoms, insist on regular medical visits, making sure that her vital signs are stable and her lab work is current. (Please see Chapter 2 for more details about medical visits.)

> Although rapport is important for any therapeutic relationship, for people with eating disorders it is especially crucial. People with EDs are often high-functioning, appearing to "have it all together." This is not necessarily true. The fact that a client with an ED is unable to do the basic human function of self-nourishment tells us she has an undeveloped and fragile self. In addition, the root of her eating disorder is a painful attachment wound. These factors make establishing a rapport paramount.

Phase 2: Manage Crisis and Core Issues

Many ED clients present with crises. Gretchen's main crisis issue (aside from her eating disorder) is substance abuse. Other crisis issues you may see with ED clients include, but are not limited to: financial instability, chronic health issues related to the ED, and major lack of family/social support.

- **Crisis/Core Issue #1: Substance Abuse**
  In addition to the questions you asked her in the initial assessment, find out whether Gretchen is a reliable reporter regarding alcohol consumption. Also, she says that her alcohol consumption increased one year ago when she became serious with her boyfriend. What was her use prior to that? Is she experiencing brownouts/blackouts? Most importantly, is she willing either to stop drinking or substantially reduce her

drinking through harm reduction during her psychotherapy treatment? Gretchen exhibits both eating-disorder and substance-abuse symptoms, so your treatment plan will depend on her answers.

If she can't utilize a harm-reduction model, you need to put the eating-disorder treatment on hold and focus on the substance abuse/chemical dependence. Refer Gretchen to a chemical-dependence (CD) treatment center. They will determine what level of care she needs for her substance-abuse problem. Many outpatient programs would permit Gretchen to work with an outside ED therapist concurrently; some will not. Managing the CD recovery by getting outside assistance will free you to focus on the ED. Interventions appropriate to this phase of treatment include: (1) **Daily Food Journal**, (2) **Food, Hunger and Satiety Log**, (3) **Evening Feelings Journal**. (Evening is the most difficult time for Gretchen as she binges after dinner. The Feelings Journal can support her in acknowledging her discomfort and heightening her awareness even as she may be engaging in the ED Behaviors.) Avoid emotionally-charged ED healing work until her CD recovery is more stable. Let her know that if she truly wants to recover from her ED she will need to stabilize her substance abuse first. The reason is twofold: Her CD behaviors lead her back to the ED, and it won't be possible to confront the emotions that fuel her ED when her CD creates a barrier to those emotions.

If she is a candidate for the harm-reduction model, contract with her weekly on the number of drinks she agrees to consume per evening on the weekend. As she responds to this intervention, decrease the number of drinks consumed over time. Though it can be terrifying for a client to relinquish both eating-disorder behaviors and alcohol, the harm-reduction model can work well for the ED client who is willing and able to use it. In addition to treating the substance abuse, harm reduction can be used to treat the ED with interventions such as the Binge-Purge Contract and Delay Binge-Purge.

It is not uncommon for a binge eater who struggles with alcohol to be a binge drinker. Explore with Gretchen how her drinking incites bingeing and purging. Later, when it is clear that Gretchen is responding to the contract work (which is emotionally neutral in nature), her ED treatment plan can include both emotionally-charged and neutral techniques.

- **Crisis/Core Issue #2: Dysthymic Disorder**
  Gretchen reports that she needed to "walk on eggshells" around her mother, and she is afraid to be candid about her eating disorder with her boyfriend. The lack of a developed sense of self that accompanies an eating disorder means that Gretchen probably did not develop the personal boundaries that would have made it safe for Gretchen to be close to others. The internal process of being attacked by her inner critic also leaves Gretchen feeling depleted and in a depressed mood.

  For this reason, the relationship she develops with you is of paramount importance. At the beginning of treatment in particular, she will be looking to you to accept and support her as you simultaneously put a boundary around the out-of-control inner critic. Gretchen's formulation of a safe connection with you becomes a model and corrective emotional experience that helps her move beyond the historical relational patterns. In addition, the relationship with you will interrupt the self-abuse she suffers at the hand of her superego, allowing Gretchen to develop an ego that can self-regulate and self-nourish. Building on the work she is doing with the psychiatrist and the medical support she is receiving, the psychotherapy component teaches the client how the loss of her voice has contributed to her depressed mood. Show her ways in which she can stand up for herself, concretizing the work you have done thus far and building a foundation for the rest of treatment by adding the following interventions: (1) **Superego Counterattacks**, (2) **Boundary-Setting Skills**, (3) any of the interventions that help the client find her voice, such as **Letter to Family Member, Letter to Inner Child/Child's Letter Back**, (4) **Feelings Drawing**. (It is a best practice, in most cases, to save potentially triggering art interventions, such as those about body image, for the third phase of treatment.)

Given her family history of emotional abandonment, and given that she hides her ED from her boyfriend, it is safe to surmise that Gretchen experiences anxiety that he will become reactive or emotionally abandoning were he to know about the bulimia. This anxiety — and the self-imposed isolation that accompanies it — drives the ED behaviors. With your help, Gretchen can determine when and if it is safe to "come out" to her boyfriend, and in which of her other friends she may confide. (Conjoint therapy with her boyfriend would be more appropriate for her in Phase 3.) Coming out of hiding will defuse the power of the ED.

Phase 3: Treat ED Behaviors Directly

The client's needs and process determine when Phase 3 begins. It can be as little as three weeks into treatment, or it can begin after many months. Assuming Gretchen's CD recovery is stable and she is able to co-create a trusting rapport with you, explore the following issues with her, using the appropriate interventions:

- **ED Issue #1: Restricting and Binge-Purge**
  As a result of her daytime restricting, Gretchen's evening binges are driven by *physical hunger* as well as emotions. Although what she eats for dinner is appropriate, signaling that she is aware of what constitutes a healthy portion, Gretchen would nevertheless benefit from seeing a dietician. That person will provide her with tools to help her move toward a nourishing diet while simultaneously fighting off ED impulses during the parts of the day when her eating is not appropriate/regulated. For instance, the dietician may suggest that Gretchen keep

large quantities of trigger foods (such as bags of cookies) out of the house for now, and purchase single-serving desserts instead.

Gretchen's binges and purges are routine and predictable: They occur in the evening after dinner, and they involve sweet foods. Since her pattern is consistent, it will be easier for you to help her confront behaviors. Any of the following interventions would be appropriate at this stage of treatment: **Alternative Choice Journal, Delay Binge-Purge, Brush Teeth, Beeline, List of Food/Exercise Rules and Rituals, Weekly Treatment Goals, Bookend Calls, Safe Relationships, Peer Support Calls** (if Safe Relationships have been established), **Faith**.

- **ED Issue #2: Body-Image Distortion**
  Gretchen's weight is within normal range but she does not see herself as normal. Her distorted body image currently aggravates the ED behaviors. She has sufficient insight to connect her poor body image with the development of her ED. Given the dynamics in her family of origin (i.e., Mom is a binge eater; the rest of the family fears Mom's anger and are conflict-avoidant; Dad is passive and Gretchen may engage in role reversal at times to take care of him; the family is a closed system), it is more likely that her preoccupation with thinness is secondary to the family-systems issues. Specifically, Gretchen experiences less stress by focusing on thinness — a tangible and concrete issue — than by digesting difficult family issues. Additionally, sometimes the ED behaviors imitate family communication styles: Mom's style ("…she never talks about feelings; she just eats all the time and then eventually blows up") is similar to the act of stuffing feelings by binge eating and then purging ("Mom blows up"). Explore with Gretchen the family dynamics and help her see how these issues directly contribute to the development of her ED. Use these interventions in conjunction with talk therapy techniques:

(1) **Superego Counterattacks**. Weave in your exploration of how her superego acts with your understanding of the family dynamics.

(2) **Three-Panel Pictures**. Explore in session how her mind interprets and distorts visual information.

(3) **Letter to My Body Part/Body Part's Response**. Since she has a rapport with you at this point, Gretchen can likely express the harsh way she talks to her body and retrieve enough compassion for herself to respond (as the body part) in an emotionally vulnerable way.

(4) **ED Timeline**. Use the timeline to investigate when and why her ED ebbed and flowed in relation to psychosocial issues and external events. Include a line depicting the relationship with her body so you can look at when and where her body distortion manifests the most. Explore verbally how cutting became a source for relief, escape, punishment, or whatever it did for her.

As this phase of treatment continues and the client feels more connected to you, use the following techniques, which are effective but which can be triggering:

(5) **Clothing Burial**
(6) **Body Tracing (for groups only)**
(7) **Alter-Image Therapy**
(8) **Contracts (like those you used in Phase 2)**

- **ED Issue #3: Compulsive Exercise**
  Gretchen has a history of exercising compulsively to compensate for her eating behaviors. Sometimes people with bulimia and EDNOS avoid exercise altogether when body-image distortion is particularly heightened. This is likely happening for Gretchen now as she refrains from exercise "because I feel too fat." Additionally, ED clients with a history of compulsive exercise — including anorexics — may experience *exercise rebellion:* disinterest in exercise as it was formerly one of

the ways in which the superego lashed the whip and now the thought of exercising is overwhelming. This results in an all-or-nothing stance on exercise. It is therefore likely that Gretchen has no concept of healthy movement and physical activity may invite compulsion in and of itself. Work with Gretchen on incorporating healthy movement into her life such as taking gentle walks to recreate an enjoyable relationship with exercise.

- **ED Issue #4: Excessive Use of Scale**
  Gretchen reports that she weighs after the evening binge-purge episodes. It is best if Gretchen stops this behavior altogether, as it is superego-driven and only serves to deplete her self-worth and increase her anxiety. If she is ready, suggest that she bring the scale in for you to hold at the office (unless she indicates that she can give it up altogether without your help). If she is not yet ready, prepare her to give up the scale by implementing a **Scale Contract**. (Like the Binge-Purge Contract, the Scale Contract supports the client to decrease the frequency with which she weighs herself. See p. 83 for more information about contracts.) Another intervention for this behavior is **Stop Thought/New Choice**, in which you will show Gretchen how to focus on something else when the compulsive thoughts about weighing start coming.

- **ED Issue #5: Part-time Job at Café**
  Is Gretchen triggered by food at her job? It is likely that her café work adds stress as it includes prolonged interaction with food. Explore this with her and help her determine whether she needs to switch to a non-food-related job. If she does, the endeavor of leaving her triggering job and finding one that is supportive to her recovery will become an effective tool for learning self-care.

- **ED Issue #6: Low Self-Esteem**
  Deepen your work with Gretchen on Superego Counterat-tacks, encouraging her to change the timbre of her internal

experience every time the superego attempts to hijack her energy. Additional interventions to raise self-esteem include: (1) **List of Positive Affirmations**; (2) **Draw Life With/Without ED**; (3) **Letter from the Treatment-Resistant Part**; (4) **Dialogue with Inner Child**; (5) **YES/NO Boundary Role Play**.

- **ED Issue #7: Perfectionism**
  A.k.a. "The Good Girl Syndrome." Notice that Gretchen's affect remains fairly bright despite her moderately depressed mood and anxiety. It is common for ED clients to assume the role of "the good girl" in order to please others and project an image of *perfection*. When the client-clinician bond is secure, it is helpful to illuminate this incongruence. In addition, you can use the **Prepare Your Defense** exercise (from Superego Counterattacks) to bring awareness of the superego's perfectionism and to challenge its authority.

Once the client feels securely connected to you, she will benefit from the following treatment techniques (which would be too complex and charged for the earlier phases): **Clothing Burial, Body Tracing** (for groups only), **Alter-Image Therapy** (from *Erasing ED* DVD), and **Contracts (Binge and/or Binge-Purge)**.

Summary of Treatment Plan

The three-phase approach is an effective way to proceed with the complicated and multi-layered issues that accompany eating disorders. To recap, the three phases are: (1) Secure Client's Safety, (2) Manage Crisis/Core Issues, and (3) Treat ED Behaviors Directly. Although each phase contains elements of ED treatment, the interventions you use will be informed by the client's level of emotional and physical stability, making each treatment plan unique.

Treatment Plan Sample Overview

1. First Phase of Treatment: Secure Client's Safety
- Comprehensive ED Assessment
- Self-Harm Assessment and No Self-Harm Contract
- Medical and Physical Evaluation

2. Second Phase of Treatment: Manage Crisis/Core Issues
- Address Substance Abuse and Dysthymia

3. Third Phase of Treatment: Treat ED Behaviors Directly
- Restricting and Binge-Purge Behaviors, Compulsive Exercise and Excessive Scale Use
- Body-Image Distortion
- Part-time Job at Café
- Low Self-Esteem

Please see the treatment plan forms for each phase on the following pages. This is a format you can use with your client to review and sign together.

Treatment Plan Phase One: Secure Client's Safety

Name: Gretchen   Date: 1/1/12

Goal	Method	Progress
1. A reduction in self-harm behaviors	Implement No Self-Harm Contract including • List of potential self-harm behaviors; • Alternative actions/sources of support.	Report progress weekly.
2. Reduction of dysthymic symptoms	Seek an evaluation for medical support for the depression • Psychiatrist OR Alternative Medicine Practitioner	
3. Good physical health	Complete monthly medical exams with M.D. • Monitor vital signs. • Keep lab work up-to-date.	

The goals above are achieved in the context of getting to know the client and her story, and establishing a secure emotional connection. The progress column indicates when to move into Phase Two. The dates listed at the top of each form are merely speculative, as you will work in concert with the client at her recovery pace.

Treatment Plan Phase Two: Manage Crisis/Core Issues

Name: Gretchen   Date: 2/1/12

Goal	Method	Progress
1. Sobriety/moderation with alcohol and other substances	• Bring consumption to non-damaging level through harm reduction OR • Achieve abstinence in chemical-dependency treatment program.	• Report progress at least bi-weekly. • Review adherence to harm-reduction contract weekly; continue to assess for higher level of CD care.
2. Stable mood	• Create safe, reliable therapeutic relationship. • Build healthy relationships with safe others. • Empower the self using Boundary-Setting Skills, Superego Counterattacks. • Retrieve the personal voice through art/writing projects: Letters to and from Family Member, Inner Child; Feelings Drawing; Positive Affirmations.	

Treatment Plan Phase Three: Treat ED Behaviors Directly

Name: Gretchen   Date: 4/1/12

Goal	Method	Progress
1. Healthy eating patterns	• Regulate eating behaviors with help from a dietician. • Replace binge-purge and restricting behaviors with other actions such as Alternative Choice Journal, Delay Binge-Purge, Brush Teeth, Beeline, List of Food/Exercise Rules and Rituals, Weekly Treatment Goals. • Seek specific personal support for challenging the ED behaviors using Bookend Calls, Safe Relationships, Peer Support Calls, Faith.	Check in and make notes on progress, at least bi-weekly. Re-visit goals weekly for level of priority and effectiveness; revise treatment plan as needed.
2. Accurate body image	• Using insights about family dynamics, identify origins of body-image distortion. • Strengthen Superego Counterattacks.	
	• Challenge visual distortions and self-critical put-downs through art and writing: Three-panel Pictures, Letter to Body Part/Body Part's Response. • Understand the ED's role in personal history through ED timeline.	
	• Explore how cutting became a source of relief in the face of the distorted body image and one of the only times that the superego was in check. • Create alignment with the self instead of the ED voice using: Clothing Burial, Alter-Image Therapy, Contracts (as in Phase 2).	

Phase Three continues on the next page.

Treatment Plan Phase Three: Treat ED Behaviors Directly (continued)

Name: Gretchen   Date: 4/1/12

Goal	Method	Progress
3. Healthy relationship with exercise	• Identify how superego has hijacked the pleasure of physical activity. • Re-create the relationship with exercise by incorporating gentle movement in small increments such as short, easy walks and dancing for pleasure.	Continue to discuss and review progress related to exercise changes, scale contracts (if applicable), and job status. Revisit former art/writing projects to illuminate progress and challenges.
4. A scale-free existence	• Implement Scale Contract. • Donate scale to charity.	
5. Non-triggering job	• Ascertain whether job at café is beneficial; seek another job if necessary.	
6. High self-esteem	• Use Superego Counterattacks as often as necessary. • Complete art/writing projects that empower the self: List of Positive Affirmations, Drawing of Life With/Without ED, Letter from the Treatment-Resistant Part, Dialogue With Inner Child, Yes/No Boundary Role Play.	

Transcribed Hypothetical Session

The following session demonstrates the techniques and theory in practice. One of the main objectives is to find out over time which interventions work best for your client, then impart them and help her apply the new skill set in her life. The behavior modifications combined with the therapeutic relationship facilitate the ultimate treatment goal: the reintegration of her id and reduction of the superego to appropriate size. This in turn allows her to regulate her emotions and nourish herself properly.

Gretchen did not have any self-harming behaviors, so Phase 1 was brief relative to many ED cases. In Phase 2, Gretchen was able to adhere to a program of harm reduction with her drinking within the context of therapy; she did not need a higher level of care. Gretchen was therefore able to move into Phase 3 by Session #7, where her ED behaviors could be treated directly. (This presumes that we have already done psycho-education about how the superego works in general, and the specific way that Gretchen's superego attacks her.) Notice how the therapist works to reintegrate the id, reduce the power of the superego, and facilitate the development of a healthy ego through the interventions and transference. What follows is a transcription of Session #8.

Phase 3, Session #8: Treating ED Behaviors Directly

Issues Addressed:

- **Transference with the therapist**
- **Challenging the ED behaviors and beliefs**
- **Chain (cycle) Analysis**
- **Superego Disengagement**

Gretchen: I'm having an awful day.

Therapist: What's going on?

Gretchen: I'm late to this session because I kept changing my clothes. I put on, like, five different things because I feel so fat. Nothing looks good. I know I must have gained weight! I'm not weighing myself right now because that's one of the treatment goals we set up, but I *know* I've gained weight and I'm freaking out!

Therapist: How do you feel about leaving the scale out of the picture for now?

Gretchen: It sucks! It was the only way of monitoring my weight before you made this treatment goal.

Therapist: So this was the only way you felt in control about your weight and size, and now that I suggested you put the scale aside for the time being, do you think you might be angry with me? *(Note how the therapist focuses on the transference/therapeutic relationship early in the session.)*

Gretchen: Oh, no! I'm not angry with you! Just at the situation…

Therapist: What if you were angry with me? Could that be okay with you?

Gretchen: I'm not though. And it would be weird. Why would I be angry at you? You're trying to help me. *(A taboo for many women, anger is especially denied in eating- disorder clients. Giving permission for her to feel and express anger increases the function of the id and decreases the power of the superego.)*

Therapist: Because I suggested a treatment goal that's hard and scary. You just told me that your scale is your safety, and I suggested we take that safety net away for now. You'd have every right to feel angry with me. *(Giving Gretchen room to have all her emotions in the therapeutic relationship, especially emotions that may have been re-pressed in the past such as anger, creates a connection with the therapist and a sense that all of Gretchen is invited into the room. The safe, reliable attachment to the therapist then makes it is easier for the client to give up reliance on her superego later in the session.)*

Gretchen: I just feel overwhelmed. And it *is* scary. Without the scale, my weight could inch up without my even knowing it. I already feel huge, so it's scary to think I could get even bigger. The only people who know how much I weigh are you and my dietician. And I'm sup-posed to learn to trust my body when I'm hungry or full? Right now all of that freaks me out.

Therapist: You're really scared.

Gretchen: Yeah.

Therapist: You're terrified that without the scale you won't be able to control your weight. *(People with eating disorders have difficulty own-ing their feelings. They may say they feel "frustrated" when they are re-ally angry, or they may say "overwhelmed" when they mean "afraid." The therapist here echoes the meaning of Gretchen's words, while taking a risk and offering Gretchen the chance to deepen her feelings.)*

Gretchen: Yeah. It's just really overwhelming.

Therapist: It sounds like you're afraid and overwhelmed, and maybe your superego is making you feel bad. Maybe you are fat with feel-ings. Does that make sense to you?

Gretchen: I don't know. I guess. But I know it's not just feelings. I see the fat too! *(When a client struggles with body-image distortion she'll want to focus on "feeling and seeing fat" rather than the feelings them-*

selves. It's important to assure her that you will allow some room for this discussion since her obsession with fat feels urgent. Over time, as real feelings surface, the need to discuss the imagined or exaggerated fat will decrease.)

Therapist: I understand you see fat. We can work with that. But what I'm wondering right now is what it feels like to rely on me, the dietician, yourself, and your body rather than the scale. What is that like for you? *(This question invites Gretchen to go deeper into the therapeutic relationship, exploring any obstacles to her reliance on the therapist.)*

Gretchen: I don't trust myself with food, so it feels crazy to rely on myself around my weight.

Therapist: So the scale would tell you if you gained or lost, and then you could adjust your food accordingly?

Gretchen: Yeah.

Therapist: How was it for you, depending on your scale all those years?

Gretchen: Awful. I hate it. I don't want to live my life around my scale.

Therapist: You don't want to eat or not eat depending on the number on your scale?

Gretchen: That's right. But not having it around is also horrible.

Therapist: Gretchen, you're the one in charge here, and I want you to remember that. Just because I suggest a treatment goal doesn't mean it's necessarily the right timing or the right goal for *you*, and it doesn't mean we have to move forward with it. You can always let me know that it's too challenging for now, or that you might not want to do it at all. *(With this reply the therapist is meeting the client "where she* *is." Although it may seem obvious that Gretchen and the therapist are in a collaborative relationship, gestures of conciliation such as this, occurring naturally in session, cannot be emphasized enough. In addition, this intervention underscores that the relationship is more important than the treatment goal of losing the scale. It also reminds the client that she has the ultimate power. This is significant, as typically the client relinquishes her power to her eating disorder. Here, the therapist illuminates the client's sense of authority.)*

Gretchen: I know that. I do want to try this—it's just hard.

Therapist: It is hard. It's really hard because it means that you'll need to start to rely on yourself rather than your scale. It means trusting yourself instead of your eating disorder. *(Having heard in Gretchen's previous response that she is indeed on board, the therapist goes to the next step, adding context by pointing out how giving up the scale fits into the larger project of recovering from the eating disorder.)*

Gretchen: Like I said, I don't know how I can rely on myself when I don't trust myself around food.

Therapist: Yes, that's the difficult part. But you don't have to do this alone. What I mean is that you have a team supporting you until you can rely on yourself. For now, you can rely on me, on your dietician, and on the group members in your Eating Disorder Process Group for another avenue of support. I want to help you understand how you can use all of us to feel safe with yourself. As you feel safer with yourself, and as you begin to see that your eating disorder doesn't really make you feel safe, you'll start to trust yourself more and more. At some point, you won't have to rely on the scale, or the eating disorder, or your inner critic for safety. *(Reminding Gretchen that she is now working in the context of a team has several powerful connotations for her and her treatment. On the one hand, it provides Gretchen a model for a healthy sense of self that is real and tangible. When she is being dominated by her own inner critic, she has a network of people whose* *strength she can "borrow" until she develops her own. In addition, the reminder that she is part of a team cuts through Gretchen's isolation and the attachment wound that is the root of the eating disorder.)*

Gretchen: Honestly, I can't even imagine that right now. I hate the scale but it's less scary to have the scale than not. *(Gretchen indicates here that she thinks the old way of being is safer than the new.)*

Therapist: Is it? Think back on how you felt after stepping on the scale in the morning, before we decided you would not weigh yourself. Can you remember how you felt? *(Tipping the scale: the therapist increases the notion that the ED voice is more of threat than recovery by using the client's own experience to get client's buy-in.)*

Gretchen: I felt disappointed, even a little panicked.

Therapist: You felt scared.

Gretchen: Yes.

Therapist: The scale brought up fear. So what did you decide to do next, on the days when you weighed yourself and were not happy with the number?

Gretchen: I would make a plan to have a really clean eating day. I was obsessed almost. I had to eat perfectly after a bad number on the scale or I wouldn't be able to concentrate. It was like someone was chasing me, looking over my shoulder. I felt under pressure.

Therapist: What would happen after that?

Gretchen: I would restrict, then I might exercise, and I would get super-hungry. Then I would eat everything that was around.

Therapist: And after that?

Gretchen: After that I would purge and then I would feel worse than ever.

Therapist: So listening to the scale set you on a track that left you feeling worse than ever. *(The therapist uses chain analysis to help Gretchen identify that each dysfunctional behavior leads her deeper into desperation and eating-disorder entrapment.)*

Gretchen: Well, if I would do things the way I'm supposed to…

Therapist: Yeah, you could have a "good" day. But the pressure is always there, if not in the foreground, then lurking in the background. Do you see how the scale is part of your eating-disorder cycle? The scale is a setup. *(Gretchen and the therapist have discussed her eating-disorder cycle in a previous session. What the therapist does now is connect the dots between the current events — Gretchen's fear of giving up the scale — and the client's personal, ongoing eating-disorder cycle.)*

Gretchen: But I feel like crap without it, too.

Therapist: Right, like when you couldn't figure out what to wear today and you felt fat?

Gretchen: Yeah.

Therapist: That's your inner critic. That's your superego. It's hanging around, and it's telling you that you are too big and you are out of control. It has you in its grip.

Gretchen: I don't know what else to do.

Therapist: Yes, that's what we were talking about before — you don't have a sense of yourself outside of the superego yet, a self that has the skill set to provide an alternative. When you reach for structure, for support, your superego shows up. But you have taken a step toward a structure that's not your superego: You have been brave enough to get rid of the scale. Gretchen, this is hard work and you're doing it. Getting rid of the scale is an action step that says, "I am going to get off the cycle of the eating disorder, this cycle that leaves me feeling miserable." Let's take it one step further now. Getting rid of the scale helps you get off the cycle outside yourself. This next step will help you get off the cycle inside yourself. Let's do Sense In and Fight Back. *(See Superego Counterattacks in the "Cognitive Behavioral Interventions" section of this chapter.)*

Gretchen: I'm not sure what you mean.

Therapist: It's that process I taught you a few weeks ago to help get your superego off your back.

Gretchen: No I mean, about the cycle inside of yourself and outside of yourself.

Therapist: When you used to weigh yourself, you would feel disappointed and anxious. The disappointment and anxiety was what inspired you to resolve to do *better* with your food that day, which eventually led to a binge. You got rid of the scale, which is great, but the part of you that makes you feel disappointed and anxious is still there, and that's your superego. So in that way, the cycle is still operating. I think that's what was happening when you couldn't figure out what to wear today.

Gretchen: I can't get rid of that; it's part of me.

Therapist: It is part of you but the way it's acting right now, it has taken you over. We're not going to get rid of it altogether. We are just going to put it back in its proper place. Once it's in its proper place, you won't be in the cycle anymore.

Gretchen: OK, I have no idea how to do that.

Therapist: I'll talk you through it. Today, nothing looked good on and you felt huge. Are you still feeling that way?

Gretchen: Less than when I came in but yeah, now that we're talking about it, it's coming back.

Therapist: How does that make you feel, to be huge? *(It is crucial that the therapist bring in the emotional element here in order illuminate Gretchen's process. As we know, "fat" is not a feeling. Gretchen's feeling of being "huge" is a reaction to a psychological process, e.g., it is a reaction to an attack by her superego. The therapist's question isolates that reaction from the superego attack itself.)*

Gretchen: Kind of anxious, and also disappointed. Under pressure.

Therapist: I remember when we did the superego work two weeks ago, "anxious" and "under pressure" were two ways you said you could tell your superego was around. So your superego must be hovering.

Gretchen: Yeah, it is definitely here.

Therapist: OK, you've just completed Step One of Sense In and Fight Back. You have noticed that you are under attack. Now, what is the superego saying?

Gretchen: It's saying that I'm fat and if I don't get a grip on myself, my body will blow up out of control.

Therapist: Right, you've identified what it's saying; that's Step Two. It's saying you're fat and you have to take measures. OK, the next step is to feel your emotional reaction to the attack. Let's be clear here, because sometimes you might be aware that you are under attack, and you might even know what it's saying — in other words, you might have done Steps One and Two — but you still might not choose to disengage. You might choose to agree with it, like, "Yeah, I am fat and I feel terrible about it."

Gretchen: That's kind of how I feel today.

Therapist: You can feel terrible and still fight back by expressing how you *really* feel when you are in the grips of your superego. That's a form of fighting back. Your feelings will inspire you not to agree with the superego, and not to rely on it. OK, one thing is, you told me you hate the scale and you don't want it running your life.

Gretchen: I do hate the scale.

Therapist: Got it. And the other thing is, you said that after a day of that cycle, of restricting and getting really hungry and binge/purging, you feel worse than ever. *(Gretchen's "home base" in today's session has been to side with the superego, identifying as "huge" and needing to be controlled. It is crucial for the therapist to help the client distinguish between feelings that are an agreement response to the superego, versus feelings that are a self-advocacy response to the superego, and then interpret this to the client. In this part of the session, the therapist directs the client to self-advocacy using Gretchen's own words and experience from today's session.)*

Gretchen: Yeah.

Therapist: So the thing to do now, once you've realized that you are under attack, and you can tell what the attack is…use the feelings about what it's really like to be in the grip of the superego. Feel how much it scares you, it pressures you, and drives you to do things that make you feel worse. OK, we're going to pretend that pillow next to you is the superego. I am going to take the voice of your superego temporarily but it's still me sitting over here. All you have to do is listen, and then "sense in" to how you are really feeling. OK, ready? *(The* *therapist reiterates that she is still connected to the client and that she will hold the boundaries.)*

Gretchen (*Sighs*): All right, I'll try it. (*Because the therapist has named and accepted the potentially scary areas earlier in the session, such as Gretchen's possible anger, she has created a safety zone in which Gretchen can own some of her id feelings — which have been too scary for her to accept and deal with on her own.)*

Therapist (*In a mean voice*): "You'd better eat well today or you're going to get bigger than you already are."

Gretchen: This is weird.

Therapist: Go ahead and let yourself feel it. "You're already so big and going to get bigger."

Gretchen: I don't know…I guess, I guess I feel anxious and hopeless.

Therapist: Say that to the pillow. Tell the superego how you're feeling.

Gretchen (*To pillow*): I feel anxious and hopeless. (*To Therapist*): This doesn't feel real.

Therapist: Sometimes these kinds of exercises can feel weird or foreign if you're not used to them; stay with me on this for a little bit. We can stop or change it if we need to, OK? (*The therapist encourages the client to go into a new emotional zone, but lets her know they are still connected. She is not going to dominate the client in order to get her to do the exercise — domination being akin to the kind of abuse that caused Gretchen's ED and which she suffers at the hands of her own superego.)*

Gretchen: OK.

Therapist: OK, I'm going to be the voice of your superego again. "You better listen to me, Gretchen! You'd better restrict today or you'll seriously get fat!" Sense in for a minute, Gretchen. How are you feeling?

Gretchen: I feel pressured. I feel upset.

Therapist: Say it to the pillow.

Gretchen (*To the pillow*): You are making me nervous.

Therapist: Good, say it again.

Gretchen: You are making me feel pressured.

Therapist: OK, can you add something now where you tell it to leave you alone?

Gretchen (*Starting to cry*): I can't tell it to leave me alone. It's my only motivation to be good around food.

Therapist: When that feels true for you, how do you feel?

Gretchen: I feel anxious and hopeless. Everything seems dark. I feel like I'm weak.

Therapist: Yes, you feel hopeless. The superego is not on your side. (*Therapist plants a seed that the superego is not a safe party with whom to be aligned.*) Stay right there with that feeling and say that.

Gretchen (*To pillow*): I feel weak and scared and you make me feel worse. (*To therapist*): I want it to go away.

Therapist: Tell it that! "I want you to go away."

Gretchen: That feels dumb.

Therapist: Just try it.

Gretchen (*To pillow*): I want you to go away.

Therapist: Good, Gretchen. Say it again.

Gretchen: I want you to go away (*starts crying again*).

Therapist: Right on. Tell it to get out of your life!

Gretchen (*Crying*): I can't do that! I wish I could.

Therapist: Then tell it anything you can for now.

Gretchen (*To pillow*): Leave me alone! You're screwing up my life!

Therapist (*Pausing*): OK. How do you feel now? (*Therapist waits so Gretchen has time to feel her feelings — the right to take up space being a major theme for Gretchen.*)

Gretchen: I feel tired. Really tired. Good in a way…not as scared.

Therapist: Do you feel less pressured? More relaxed?

Gretchen: Yeah, I don't feel like I'm being chased right now.

Therapist: Good. You did it. You told the superego the truth and moved out of the cycle. (*Therapist ties experiential work back to psycho-education [chain analysis] work.*) Well done. (*Note here that the client thinks she can't disengage from the superego, but when it's broken down into something she is <u>allowed to feel</u> instead of something she <u>has to do</u>, she can, in fact, disengage. The matter at hand is not to do something as much as it to have permission to feel something. This harks back to the beginning of the session when the therapist gave the client permission to feel anger about the scale being taken away. Her experience*

*of having had permission to be angry and knowing that "anger is safe"
adds to Gretchen's sense of feeling safe to express her feelings now.)*

Gretchen: Yeah, thanks.

Therapist: So this is what it looks and feels like to stand up to your superego.

Gretchen: But I couldn't tell it to get out of my life like you said. *(Gretchen's superego comes in quickly to tell her she was still inadequate. The therapist's role then is to help her reconnect with her triumph — not at the therapist's insistence, but by the therapist helping Gretchen reconnect with herself.)*

Therapist: It's one step at a time. What you did was very powerful and effective. You stood your ground, Gretchen. Have you ever done that before? *(This question reconnects Gretchen with her experience — with what just happened. It also increases her faith in success with new treatment interventions.)*

Gretchen: Actually, no. I guess I always let it take the lead.

Therapist: Well this time you didn't. You just took an important step toward having a reliable self. This is the other part of getting rid of the scale. Are you giving yourself credit right now? *(Brings attention to Gretchen's internal victory, but from her perspective, not the therapist's.)*

Gretchen (*smiling*): Yeah. I guess so. Yeah.

Therapist: Is it okay if we shift gears for a moment and prep you for later on, just in case you start to feel triggered?

Gretchen: Sure.

Therapist: When do you usually feel like bingeing and purging?

Gretchen: After dinner.

Therapist: OK so why don't you do Bookend Calls? *(See "Interpersonal Techniques" in the "Treatment Tools and Techniques" section of this chapter.)* Leave me a voicemail before dinner and tell me what you plan to eat for dinner, your Hunger Level, and how you're feeling in that moment. After dinner, call me with your Satiety Level, how you're feeling and your post-meal plan: for example, "I'm going to "beeline" to my bedroom, read a book or journal, then wash up and go to bed." How does this Bookend plan feel?

Gretchen: Good, but I don't want to disturb you. *(Again, the superego tells Gretchen she's too big/taking up too much space. The therapist then can reassure her where the boundaries are.)*

Therapist: It won't disturb me, I will just listen to the message and that's it. I won't call you back unless you tell me it's an emergency, and then I would. OK?

Gretchen: OK.

Therapist: All right, then I'll hear from you tonight.

Gretchen: Ok, that sounds good.

Therapist: See you next week, Gretchen.

Gretchen: Bye.

To review, the clinical issues addressed in this session were: transference, challenging the ED beliefs and behaviors, and implementing the use of Chain Analysis and Superego Disengagement. The therapist created a safe environment in which Gretchen could experience her feelings (anger, fear, etc.), supporting the id and rightsizing the superego. Additionally, the therapist provided helpful treatment tools for the client's benefit inside and outside of session. Treating the eating disorder directly, Phase 3, was the appropriate therapeutic focus given the client's status.

CONCLUSION

The overarching message of *Erasing ED* — the movie and the manual — is that full recovery from eating disorders is possible. It requires psychological wisdom and creative orchestration on the part of the therapist, and profound bravery on the part of the client. Here are some highlights of the treatment philosophy:

- Expect to do both cognitive behavioral and psychodynamic work in the same course of treatment.
- Tailor your use of interventions to each client. Interventions that work for some do not work for others.
- A team approach is the best practice — a clinically sound way to care for your client and yourself. EDs require expertise from a variety of specialists: the M.D., the dietician, the psychiatrist, and a recovery community, in addition to the therapist.
- Do not underestimate the impact of the superego on these disorders. Be ready to support your client to disengage whenever necessary.
- The integration of the id (e.g., allowing it to become part of consciousness) and the rightsizing of the superego empower the ego. The robust ego then becomes a source of strength the client can use to regulate her emotions and nourish herself.

We offer these parting words from Georgia O'Keeffe, a call to integrate the id: "I decided that if I could paint that flower in a huge scale, you could not ignore its beauty."

Photo Credit: Newark Museum / Art Resource, NY

Georgia O'Keeffe, *White Flower on Red Earth No. 1*. Oil on canvas, 26 x 30 in. Newark Museum, Newark, New Jersey.

APPENDIX A

Assessment Form

e r a s i n g **E D**

Comprehensive Eating Disorders Assessment

1. Client Demographics

Name _____ Assessment date _____ D.O.B._____

Client contact information _____

Gender _____ Ethnicity _____ Sexual orientation _____

Employment and/or school _____

Primary source of income _____

Insurance information (if applicable) _____

Relationship status _____ Referral source _____

Emergency contact _____

Five-Axis Diagnosis _____

_____ Rule out _____

2. Treatment History

Psychiatrists, Psychologists, Psychotherapists _____

_____

_____

Dieticians/Nutritionists _____

Treatment programs _____

Hospitalizations _____

Twelve-Step experience _____

3. Medical History

Name of M.D. _____

Date of last M.D. appointment; reason for appointment _____

List of current medication(s) and doses _____

Significant medical history _____

Date of last menses _____ Does M.D. know about client's eating issues? _____

Date of last dental appointment _____ Does dentist know about client's eating issues? _____

Continued on next page

4. Self-harm and Violence History

Self-harming behaviors _____

_____ Dates _____

Suicidal ideation _____ Dates _____

Suicide attempts _____ Dates _____

Homicidal ideation _____ Dates _____

Violence toward others _____ Dates _____

5. Abuse History

Emotional or verbal abuse _____

Physical abuse _____

Sexual abuse: rape and/or date rape _____

Domestic violence _____

Emotional neglect/abandonment _____

6. Specific Eating Disorder Information and Behaviors

Present weight and height _____ Highest weight and age _____

Lowest weight and age (lowest adult weight if treating an adult) _____

Individual's report of "ideal" weight _____ Frequency of weighing _____

Eating-disorder-related complications (e.g., acid reflux, blood in vomit or stool, knee problems) _____

_____

_____

Current and past behaviors (include dates):

   ❑ Binge eating _____

   ❑ Compulsive overeating _____

   ❑ Restricting _____

   ❑ Fasting (such as a "juice only" fast) _____

   ❑ Vomiting _____

   ❑ Dieting _____

   Diet aids (check all that apply and include dates of use): ❑ Pills_____ ❑ Laxatives_____

   ❑ Diuretics_____ ❑ Ipecac_____ ❑ Enemas_____

   ❑ Supplements _____

Continued on next page

❑ Compulsive exercise (frequency, intensity, and duration; and is it compensatory?) _____

❑ Chewing and spitting _____

❑ Eating late at night/in middle of night _____

❑ Hoarding or hiding food _____

❑ Counting calories/making caloric lists _____

❑ Cutting food into small pieces _____

❑ Creating rules and/or rituals _____

❑ Compulsive self-weighing _____

❑ Preoccupation with weight, body size _____

❑ Eating an ultra-pure diet (e.g., restricting fats, proteins, carbohydrates, only eating vegetables or fruits, etc.) _____

_____

List of behaviors above that occurred in the past six months _____

_____

_____

List of behaviors above that occurred in the past month _____

_____

_____

Description of binges (content, location) _____

_____

_____

List of "safe" foods _____

_____

_____

7. Family History

Eating disorders _____

Chemical dependency and/or abuse _____

Mental health issues or illness _____

Physical illness _____

Continued on next page

Genogram (draw below)

8. Onset and Duration of Eating Disorder

Individual's detailed report of when and why the ED began _____

_____

_____

_____

_____

9. List of Food Consumed on a Typical Day

Date, time, food content, quantity for each meal/snack/episode. _____

_____

_____

_____

_____

Continued on next page

10. Chemical Dependency (CD) History

Name of substance(s) including all alcohol and drugs _____

_____

_____

Duration of use, including frequency and greatest amounts consumed_____

_____

_____

_____

Last use (date and amount)_____ Age of onset_____

CD treatment and Twelve-Step history_____

_____

11. History of Other Compulsive Behaviors

Duration, freqency of each: sex and love addiction, gambling, excessive spending or debting, under-spending, self-deprivation.

_____

_____

12. Support System

A list of family/friends with whom the individual feels safe and supported, along with a list of anyone who knows about his/her eating disorder (and substance abuse, if applicable).

_____

_____

13. Client's Expectations of Treatment

Individual's expectation of treatment, including what he/she wants to change or accomplish. _____

_____

_____

14. Result of Interview/Clinician's Recommendations

Reported findings, diagnoses, clinical suggestions and concerns. _____

_____

_____

ARTISTS' STATEMENTS

Nicole Laby
Paintings: (1) *Smothered*; (2) *Ontogeny*; (3) *In Flight*
Medium: Oil on canvas with charcoal and coarse pumice gel.

This trilogy chronicles the eating disorder recovery process. I was inspired to create this work by the memory of my own recovery from anorexia and bulimia many years ago, and from the recovery I help to facilitate in my work with eating-disordered clients.

"Smothered" illustrates the initial stage of recovery, when every inch of space is consumed with anger, fear, and the dominating superego. Raw slivers of canvas peering through indicate vulnerability, and layered brush strokes communicate the frenzied psyche.

"Ontogeny" captures the middle stage of recovery, when the pieces of the healthy psyche begin to appear more clearly. The ultimate transformation of *parts into whole* is expressed in roughly formed circles evolving into a single circle.

"In Flight" is the synthesis of the previous recovery stages. The ascending wing-like arches mark the departure from the constraints of the superego and the embrace of the authentic self.

Sheira Kahn
Poems in response to paintings

These paintings remind me of the intense, seemingly endless pain of eating disorders, and the unexpected, delicious freedom that comes when they depart, even for a moment. In the final poem, I wanted to emphasize the hallmark of healing: that a person has the right to take up space and belong in the world as a full-fledged, connected member of creation.

The Arts help me find meaning and purpose in recovery, even when events seem random and without virtue. Writing, dance and visual art have been available, like good friends, whenever I remember to reach out for their healing power and perspective. Nicole and I are pleased that art and poetry have a place in this manual, a partner to scholarship.

RESOURCES

Nicole Laby, MFT
Licensed Psychotherapist MFC #43780
www.ErasingED.com
www.NicoleLaby.com

2261 Market St., Suite 422
San Francisco, CA 94114
415-820-3952

For information on eating-disorder consultation and *Erasing ED* (the movie), go to www.ErasingED.com.

Sheira Kahn, MFT
Licensed Psychotherapist MFC #40344
www.SheiraKahn.com
www.CEUcinema.com

1728 Union St., Suite 210
San Francisco, CA 94123

705 Fourth St., Suite 200
San Rafael, CA 94901
415-336-4631

For information on classes about Superego Disengagement, go to www.SheiraKahn.com. For continuing education classes on eating

disorders and other subjects pertinent to today's mental health practitioner, go to www.CEUcinema.com.

Avril Swan, M.D.

www.wholefamilymd.org
1286 Sanchez Street, Suite A
San Francisco, CA 94114
415-642-0333

Something Fishy
Comprehensive eating-disorder information
www.something-fishy.org

ED Referral
Database of ED Professionals
www.edreferral.com

National Eating Disorders Association (NEDA)
National nonprofit eating-disorders organization offering information, referrals, support, prevention, conferences, and newsletters
www.edap.org

**National Association of Anorexia Nervosa and Associated Disor-
ders (ANAD)**
Nonprofit organization that provides details of support programs
and volunteer opportunities
www.anad.org

Gurze Books
Books, newsletters, treatment referrals, and clearinghouse of general
information on eating disorders
www.bulimia.com

Index

ABOUT THE AUTHORS

Nicole Laby, MFT, has been treating eating disorders for nearly two decades and teaches recovery methods to graduate students and fellow clinicians. She lives in Oakland, California with her husband and two children.

Sheira Kahn, MFT, is a psychotherapist in private practice who teaches classes on eating disorders and psychology to clinicians and recovering addicts. A founder of www.CEUcinema.com, she lives in the San Francisco Bay Area.